Austrian Desserts
and Pastries

First edition published 2010 Residenz Verlag
Part of Niederösterreichischen Pressehaus
Druck- und Verlagsgesellschaft mbH
St. Pölten - Salzburg

Skyhorse Publishing books may be purchased in bulk at special discounts for
sales promotion, corporate gifts, fund-raising, or educational purposes. Special
editions can also be created to specifications. For details, contact the Special
Sales Department, Skyhorse Publishing, 307 West 36th Street, 11th Floor,
New York, NY 10018 or info@skyhorsepublishing.com.

Skyhorse® and Skyhorse Publishing® are registered trademarks of
Skyhorse Publishing, Inc.®, a Delaware corporation.

www.skyhorsepublishing.com

10 9 8 7 6 5 4 3 2 1

Library of Congress Cataloging-in-Publication Data is available on file.
ISBN: 978-1-61608-399-1

Printed in China

DIETMAR FERCHER   ANDREA KARRER

Austrian Desserts and Pastries

108 Classic Recipes

Translated by Erik Werner
Photography by Konrad Limbeck
Illustrations by Barbara Kampel

Skyhorse Publishing

Contents

The Sweet Life . . .

Since the nineteenth century, Viennese confectioners have been world-renowned, and even today Vienna remains a fertile ground for culinary careers. The pastry kitchens have retained their traditions while at the same time always remaining receptive to new influences. The unparalleled abundance and wealth of variations that has resulted is practically unique among cuisines.

My sweet tooth has always forced me to succumb to the many pleasures awaiting me in Vienna's pastry heaven.

For a long time, I mourned the irresistible pastries that used to be at the Imperial, until I found out that the former pastry chef of the Imperial group had gone into business on his own. Now he's among the very best Viennese confectioners. Dietmar Fercher's crisp *Schaumrollen* (cream rolls), delicate *Schaumschnitten* (cream cakes), and fluffy *Golatschen* (kolache pastries) have revolutionized the confectionery of our time with their almost therapeutic effects.

It took my eating a lot of cream cakes at the small confectioner's on *Engerthstrasse* until Dietmar finally promised to rework his recipes and to write a Viennese pastry book with me.

He revealed about 180 recipes to me, and Konrad Limbeck has created atmospheric photographs to match. Since I am of the belief that the origin of many a recipe often tells you more about historical contexts than some scientific treatises can, I have made the traditional division into cold and warm pastries. This will also allow you to learn about the origins of some of the dishes.

This background is complemented by professional tips and important basic skills from the bakery to enable you to easily follow

Dietmar Fercher's pastry baking recipes. All recipes were baked in normal household quantities, amended, revised, and tested again, to ensure they truly do work. Wherever greater attention is necessary, Barbara Kampel contributes to easier comprehension with her beautiful illustrations.

One more piece of important advice: before preparing a pastry, make sure to read the entire recipe carefully. Only then follow it step by step, ounce by ounce. If you follow this procedure, you can be sure of successfully preparing every dessert in this book.

Andrea Karrer

PS: Not just the cream cakes, but also the plump cranberry *Guglhupf* (ring cake) and the (best!) apple crumb cake had to be devoured. Oh yes, and the *Krapfen* (donuts) at carnival, *Marillenknödel* (apricot dumplings) in July, countless *Plunder* (Danish pastries) for breakfast, then of course the occasional banana and raspberry cream cakes, and the puff pastries I only recognized from childhood memories, and delicacies such as *Rigó Jancsischnitten* (special cake named for a gypsy violinist), and the list goes on . . .

Warm
Mehlspeisen

Strudel

It's practically the Austrian national dish, but like much of what became part of Viennese cuisine, strudel is also an "immigrant," and quite the well-traveled one at that: The Arabs were the first to practice the art of stretching out paper-thin sheets of dough, filling them with rose jelly or orange syrup, and baking them. Nor did they want to miss out on this tender delicacy when out conquering. Whether in northern Africa, Spain, or western Africa, wherever the Arabs advanced, strudel went native. In antique cookbooks, you can still find strudel dough under the name "Spanish dough." However, the Moors of Spain did not roll up the strudel dough, but rather laid alternating layers of dough and filling atop one another. Baklava, originating from Turkey and extremely popular in the Balkans, is prepared according to this principle as well.

The paper-thin pastry sheets accompanied the Arabs' triumphal entrance into France. When the Arabs returned to their homeland after their defeat at the Battle of Poitiers, the liberated countries retained the skill of baking strudel, but it did not spread any farther. The strudel was preserved as "*Pastis*" or "*Croustade*" and potentially could even have been assimilated into the Austrian cuisine along with many other French specialties. As a matter of fact though, it was brought by the Turks. They advanced via the Balkans to Hungary and Vienna, and in their field kitchens wreaths of aromatic strudel could be found, which stayed on after the siege of Vienna as a gift from the Orient. Hungary, where strudel is known as "*retes*," must have been quite the special stopover. For here an especially sticky flour could be found that made the dough very malleable. Thus western Hungary (present-day Burgenland), Vienna, and Lower Austria were the first areas where strudel became widespread. Here you can also find the greatest variety of fillings.

In Vienna it is said that a conscientious strudel baker stretches out the dough so thin that she can read her love letters through it. This led to the saying that the best strudel is baked by a cook who is in love.

Today of course you can buy strudel dough ready-made, a true delight. But if you ever bake strudel for someone you're especially fond of, you should try making the strudel dough yourself for a change so that you can pour out your heart not just into the filling, but also into the whisper-thin sleeve.

Packing filling into strudel dough is the most natural thing in the world to us today. It's a brilliant concept! In this fashion, the juice from the fruit or other ingredients can't leak (provided of course the strudel is made correctly). The preservation of the juice keeps things moist during the baking process and in the finished strudel as well.

Tips

- Use fine flour for strudel dough.
- It is essential that the dough rest for at least 30 minutes so that it can relax and the glutens in the dough can develop.
- When baking strudel dough, an egg or egg yolk must be added.
- The work step that requires the most attention is the stretching. It is not difficult, but some tips should be followed. In most cases, the dining table must serve for stretching out the dough. Don't forget to put down a large linen sheet to protect the floor.
- Use a light-colored, washable tablecloth for the strudel cloth—no damask! The filling could leave stains.
- Check fingernails and remove rings so that the dough doesn't tear.
- The best thing is to first roll out the dough as a rectangle, then gently lift the dough from underneath with the floured backs of the hands and gradually stretch it thinner to the desired size.
- In order to give the filling more "hold" and make sure it's well wrapped in the dough, do not spread it over the entire dough surface, but instead only on the lower third, leaving a margin of about 2 $1/3$ inches (6 cm).
- Cut away thick outer dough edges with a sharp knife.
- Toss the end of the dough over the filling, pinch off the side lengths, and pull them over the filling a bit.
- Slightly lift the strudel cloth and tightly roll the strudel with the help of the cloth.
- Lift the strudel cloth containing the strudel at both ends and let it slide from the cloth onto a greased baking sheet (or lined with parchment paper).

Important: If not using parchment paper: remove baked strudel from the sheet as soon as possible. If it rests on a (non-enameled) sheet for too long, the strudel will get a "metallic" taste.

If you're in a hurry, there's no shame in using store-bought strudel dough sheets. They are an excellent alternative to homemade strudel dough.

Even without the preparation of the dough, there are a few things to remember:
- The strudel cloth should ideally consist of two cloths: one lower damp one and one upper dry one.
- It's a good idea to spread some melted butter between the dough sheets.
- Don't spread the filling to the edges.
- Make sure to have some reserve strudel dough at the ready in case your dough tears.

Basic Recipe Stretched Strudel Dough

Yields 10 servings
(as dessert)

3 cups (300 g) flour (fine)
approximately 1 ounce
(30 ml) ($\frac{1}{8}$ cup or 30 g oil
a pinch of salt
approximately ¾ cup ($\frac{3}{16}$ l)
of water
flour for preparing
oil for brushing

Sift the flour onto a work surface. Make a well in the center and pour in oil, salt, and about ¾ of the amount of water. Using two dough scrapers, mix from the outside in, and then knead with your hands into a smooth, supple dough.
Note: The exact amount of water depends on the gluten content of the flour; a little water may have to be added. Form dough into a ball, place on a floured plate, brush with oil, and let rest covered in a warmed bowl at room temperature for about 1 hour. Sprinkle a "strudel cloth" with flour. Sprinkle the dough with flour, roll out just under ½ inch thick, and pull out the dough using the backs of the hand to the desired size. Brush with melted butter, cover or spread with filling. Cut away thick outer dough edges with a sharp knife. Fold over the sides and tightly roll up the dough with the help of the strudel cloth. Place on a greased baking sheet (or lined with parchment paper), brush with melted butter, and bake.

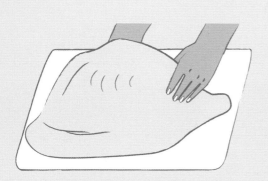

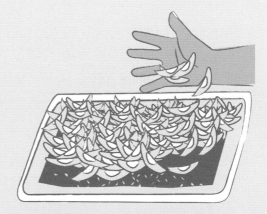

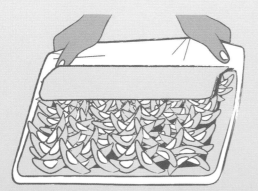

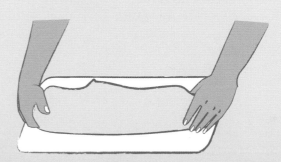

Sweet Cream Strudel

Topfen is the Austrian version of the German *Quark*, a type of curd cheese that can be used in dishes both sweet and savory.

Prepare homemade strudel dough according to the basic recipe and let rest.

Filling: Separate eggs. Pass *Topfen* through a sieve using a dough scraper. Stir soft butter together with lemon peel, powdered and vanilla sugar, and a pinch of salt until creamy. Alternate stirring *Topfen* and yolk into the butter mix. Beat egg whites with granulated sugar until stiff. Stir $1/_3$ of the egg whites with the sour cream into the *Topfen* mix. Fold in the remaining egg whites, alternating with flour.

Stretch out the homemade strudel dough according to the basic recipe. If using store-bought strudel dough: place two store-bought strudel dough sheets onto a damp cloth so that they overlap slightly, and brush with some melted butter (including the strip of dough located under the "overlap"). Cut apart a third strudel sheet and place it onto the two other sheets so that the area consists of a double layer of dough throughout. Brush dough with butter.

Place filling on the lower third and roll up the strudel with the help of the cloth. Place strudel in a buttered baking dish (preferably loaf-shaped). Important: The strudel must fill the pan, otherwise it will fall apart. Bake in preheated oven at 310°F (155°C) for about 15 minutes.

Topping: Stir together milk and eggs, granulated and vanilla sugar, then pour evenly over strudel and bake an additional 35 minutes until done. Remove from the oven, brush with remaining butter, and let cool about 20 minutes.

In the meantime, prepare vanilla sauce according to the recipe on p. 259. Cut sweet cream strudel into servings, remove from the pan, sprinkle with powdered sugar, and serve with vanilla sauce.

Yields 8 servings

Strudel Dough:
Basic recipe (p. 14) or
3 store-bought strudel dough
sheets

Filling:
4 eggs
1 ½ cups (350 g) *Topfen* *
½ cup (100 g) soft butter
peel of ½ lemon (untreated),
zested
¾ cup (30 g) powdered sugar
1 tsp vanilla sugar
salt
$1/_3$ cup (70 g) granulated sugar
2 cups (¼ l) sour cream
$1/_3$ cup (30 g) flour (fine)
about ½ cup (100 g) melted
butter
Butter for the mold

Topping:
$2/_3$ cup (150 ml) milk
2 eggs
1 tbsp granulated sugar
1 tsp vanilla sugar

Vanilla Sauce:
See recipe, p. 259
Powdered sugar for sprinkling

Apple Strudel

Strudel Dough:
Basic recipe (p. 14) or
3 store-bought strudel dough
sheets
about ½ cup (100 g) melted
butter for brushing

Filling:
²/₃ cup (100 g) raisins
2 ½ pounds (1.20 kg) tart apples (such as Boskoop, Elstar,
Rennette) juice and zested
peel of 1 lemon (untreated)
mixed with a little sugar
½ cup (100 g) granulated
sugar or brown sugar
2 tsp vanilla sugar
pinch of cinnamon (ground)

Butterbrösel:
120 g Butter
150 g Semmelbrösel
1 MS Zimt
1 TL Vanillezucker
2 EL Kristallzucker

Staubzucker zum Bestreuen

If using homemade strudel dough, prepare it according to the basic recipe and let rest.

Filling: Wash raisins in hot water and drain well in a colander. Peel apples, quarter, core, and—preferably with a vegetable slicer—slice into thin slices. In a bowl, thoroughly combine apples with granulated sugar (**note:** the exact amount of sugar depends on the acid content of the type of apple), cinnamon, vanilla sugar, lemon zest and juice, and raisins.

Buttered Bread Crumbs: Melt butter. Brown crumbs in butter together with cinnamon, vanilla sugar, and granulated sugar. Add half the amount of buttered crumbs to the apple filling.

Place two store-bought strudel dough sheets onto a damp cloth so that they overlap slightly, brush with some melted butter (including the strip of dough located under the "overlap"). Cut apart a third strudel sheet and place onto the two other sheets so that the area consists of a double layer of dough throughout. Sprinkle remaining buttered crumbs on the bottom third of the dough area. Brush remaining dough area with a little melted butter. Spread apple filling onto the buttered crumbs, tightly roll up the strudel with the help of the strudel cloth, press strudel ends closed, and cut away excess dough; using the strudel cloth, place strudel onto a baking sheet lined with parchment paper. Brush with butter and bake in a preheated oven at 410°F (210°C) for about 25–30 minutes. Remove strudel from oven, brush with remaining butter, cut into servings, and sprinkle with powdered sugar.

Serve apple strudel warm or cold.

Pear Strudel with Williams Sauce

Yields 8 servings

Strudel Dough:
Basic recipe (p. 14) or 3 store-bought strudel dough sheets

Filling:
1 ¾ lbs (800 g) pears (preferably Bartlett, known as Williams Christ pears in Austria)
$1/_3$ cup (50 g) raisins
4 cl (2–3 tbsp) of Williams brandy (Austrian spirit distilled from Williams pears)
2 tbsp granulated sugar
pinch of cinnamon
juice of ½ a lemon
about 5 ounces (150 g) of milk loaf, brioche, or *Biskuit* slices*

Williams Sauce:
See recipe (p. 259)
about ½ cup (100 g) melted butter
powdered sugar for sprinkling

Biskuit is best.

Prepare homemade strudel dough according to the basic recipe and let rest.

Filling: Wash pears, peel, cut in quarters, and remove cores. Cut pears thinly. Wash raisins in hot water and drain well on absorbent paper. Mix pear slices well with raisins, Williams brandy, granulated sugar, cinnamon, and lemon juice and let stand for about 10 minutes.

Remove crusts from milk loaf or brioche and cut into ½ inch (1 ½ cm) cubes, then mix in with the pears.

Stretch out the homemade strudel dough according to the basic recipe. If using store-bought strudel dough: Place two store-bought strudel dough sheets onto a damp cloth so that they overlap slightly, and brush with some melted butter (including the strip of dough located under the "overlap"). Cut apart a third strudel sheet and place onto the two other sheets so that the area consists of a double layer of dough throughout. Brush dough with butter.

Spread filling onto the bottom third and roll up the strudel with the help of the cloth, press the outer edges closed, pinch off and cut away excess dough; using the cloth, place strudel onto a baking sheet lined with parchment paper. Brush with butter and bake in a preheated oven at 410°F (205°C) for about 20–25 minutes.

Prepare Williams Sauce: According to the recipe on p. 259. Remove strudel from oven, cut into servings, sprinkle with powdered sugar, and serve with Williams sauce.

Rhubarb Strudel with Almond Sauce

Prepare homemade strudel dough according to the basic recipe and let rest.

Buttered Bread Crumbs: Melt butter. Brown crumbs in butter together with cinnamon, vanilla sugar, and granulated sugar.

Filling: Wash and peel the rhubarb, cut into ¾ inch (2 cm) pieces. Wash raisins in hot water and drain well on absorbent paper. Mix rhubarb with brown sugar, raisins, almonds, and cinnamon.

Stretch out the homemade strudel dough according to the basic recipe. If using store-bought strudel dough: Place two store-bought strudel dough sheets onto a damp cloth so that they overlap slightly, and brush with some melted butter (including the strip of dough located under the "overlap"). Cut apart a third strudel sheet and place onto the two other sheets so that the area consists of a double layer of dough throughout. Spread butter crumbs on the bottom third. Brush remaining dough area with melted butter. Spread filling onto the butter crumbs and roll up the strudel with the help of the cloth, press the outer edges closed, pinch off and cut away excess dough; using the cloth, place strudel onto a baking sheet lined with parchment paper. Brush with butter and bake in a preheated oven at 400°F (200°C) for about 25–30 minutes.

Prepare almond sauce according to the recipe on p. 257. Remove strudel from oven, brush with remaining butter, cut into servings, sprinkle with powdered sugar, and serve with almond sauce.

Yields 8 servings

Strudel Dough:
Basic recipe (p. 14) or 3 store-bought strudel dough sheets

Buttered bread crumbs:
heaping ½ cup (120 g) butter
2 cups (150 g) bread crumbs
pinch of cinnamon
1 tsp vanilla sugar
1 tbsp granulated sugar

Filling:
2 ¼ lbs (1 kg) rhubarb (hot-house rhubarb tastes best)
$^2/_3$ cup (100 g) raisins
1 cup (80 g) almonds, roasted and grated
about 1 cup (200 g) brown sugar
pinch of cinnamon (ground)
about ½ cup (80 g) melted butter

Almond Sauce:
See recipe (p. 257)

Grape Strudel

Yields 8-10 servings

Strudel Dough:
Basic recipe (p. 14) or 3 store-bought strudel dough sheets
a little over ½ cup (120 g) melted butter

Filling:
1 ¾ lbs (750 g) grapes (preferably seedless)
3 eggs
$^1/_3$ cup (70 g) granulated sugar
pinch of salt
1 tsp vanilla sugar
pinch of cinnamon (ground)
½ cup (50 g) flour (fine)
$^2/_3$ cup (50 g) walnuts, ground

Wine Sauce:
Recipe (p. 259)

If using homemade strudel dough, prepare it according to the basic recipe and let rest. Meanwhile, prepare the filling.

Filling: Wash grapes, remove stems, and drain well. Separate eggs. Beat yolk with $^1/_3$ of the granulated sugar, salt, and vanilla sugar until creamy. Beat egg whites with remaining sugar until soft peaks form. Mix cinnamon with flour. Stir $^1/_3$ of the egg whites into the yolk mixture. Then fold in remaining egg whites, walnuts, and cinnamon flour.

Stretch out the homemade strudel dough according to the basic recipe, brush with butter, spread on filling, then proceed according to the basic recipe.

Place two store-bought strudel dough sheets onto a damp cloth so that they overlap slightly, and brush with some melted butter (including the strip of dough located under the "overlap"). Cut apart a third strudel sheet and place onto the two other sheets so that the area consists of a double layer of dough throughout. Brush with butter. Spread filling onto the bottom third and evenly distribute grapes onto the nut mixture. Tightly roll up the strudel with the help of the strudel cloth, press strudel ends closed, and cut away excess dough. Using the strudel cloth, place strudel onto a baking sheet lined with parchment paper. Brush with butter and bake in a preheated oven at 375°F (190°C) for about 30 minutes.

Wine Sauce: Prepare according to the recipe on p. 259.

Remove strudel from oven, cut into servings, and serve with wine sauce.

Cooked Semolina Strudel with Black Currant Sauce

Yields 6 servings

Strudel Dough:
Add 1 yolk to the basic recipe
(p. 14) *
a little over ½ cup (120 g)
melted butter

Filling:
¼ cup (50 g) *Topfen* (10% fat)
2 eggs
3 tbsp (40 g) softened butter
pinch of salt
zest of ½ a lemon (untreated)
¼ cup (50 ml) sour cream
½ cup (90 g) wheat semolina
2 ½ tbsp (30 g) granulated
sugar
about 1 cup (100 g) butter
crumbs (see recipe, page 24)

*Of course you can also prepare
the cooked Semolina Strudel with
store-bought strudel dough, but
it turns out much better with
homemade dough.

Prepare homemade strudel dough according to the basic recipe with one extra egg yolk and let rest. Meanwhile, prepare the filling.

Filling: Press *Topfen* through a sieve with a dough scraper. Separate eggs. Stir softened butter with salt and lemon zest until creamy. Gradually stir in yolk and *Topfen*. Stir in sour cream and semolina. Let mixture rest for about 1 ½ hours. Beat egg whites with granulated sugar until stiff and fold into the semolina mixture.

Stretch out strudel dough on floured cloth. Spread filling in the lower third about 4 inches wide. Brush remaining dough area with melted butter. Cut away thick outer dough edges. Roll up the strudel not too tightly with the help of the strudel cloth Using a floured wooden spoon, press off portions (4 inches long), and cut with a knife. Pinch the ends off tightly. Bring plenty of water to boil with a little salt, put in Strudel packages, and let stand for about 15 minutes nearly covered over low heat, turning once. Remove strudel pieces from the water and drain; cut semolina strudel in a little over ½ inch (1 ½ cm) thick pieces and serve with currant sauce (see recipe, p. 259). Sprinkle with butter crumbs (see recipe, p. 24).

Tip: Poached pears go very well with the cooked semolina strudel.

Small Plum Strudel with Cinnamon Sauce

Yields 6 servings

Strudel Dough:
Basic recipe (p. 14) or 3 store-bought strudel dough sheets
a little over ½ cup (120 g) melted butter

Cinnamon Sauce:
1 cup (¼ l) milk
$^1/_3$ cup (70 g) granulated sugar
1 tsp vanilla sugar
pinch of salt
2 cinnamon sticks
about 1 tsp of vanilla pudding powder
1 egg yolk

Buttered Bread Crumbs:
3 ½ tbsp (50 g) butter
1 cup (60 g) bread crumbs
1 small pinch of cinnamon
1 tbsp granulated sugar

Filling:
just over a pound (½ kg) of ripe, not too watery plums (best are damson plums)
pinch of cinnamon (ground)
2 tbsp plum schnapps (slivovitz)
¼ cup (50 g) granulated sugar
1 cup (80 g) walnuts, ground

Powdered sugar for sprinkling

Prepare homemade strudel dough according to the basic recipe and let rest.

Sauce: Bring ¼ cup (1/16 l) of milk to a boil with granulated and vanilla sugars, salt, and cinnamon sticks, remove from heat, and let stand for about 10 minutes. Blend remaining milk with vanilla pudding powder and egg yolk. Remove cinnamon sticks from milk, bring to a boil again, and stir the vanilla egg yolk milk into the cinnamon milk. Cook sauce while constantly stirring until the sauce thickens. Allow to cool and chill.

Buttered Bread Crumbs: Melt butter, stir in bread crumbs, cinnamon, and granulated sugar, and roast while stirring; remove from heat.

Filling: Wash plums, remove stones, and drain well. Cut plums into quarters; mix in a bowl with cinnamon, brandy, and sugar, and let sit for 10 minutes. Mix walnuts and $^1/_3$ of the butter crumbs with the plums.

Stretch out the strudel dough according to the basic recipe or place the store-bought strudel dough on damp cloths. Cut the strudel dough so that two rectangular dough sheets result, brush these with a little melted butter, sprinkle with remaining butter crumbs, and spread filling on each rectangle in three portions which apply (for store-bought strudel dough sheets use two portions filling for each dough sheet). Roll up the strudel with the help of the cloth, pinch off the dough between portions using the fingertips, and cut into six small strudel. Fold the ends and press firmly closed.

Place strudel onto a baking sheet lined with parchment paper, brush with remaining melted butter, and bake in preheated oven at 400°F (200°C) for about 15 minutes. **Note:** The exact cooking time depends on the type of plums.

Sprinkle strudel with powdered sugar and serve with cinnamon sauce (recipe, p. 259).

Small Date Strudel with Coffee Sauce

Yields 4 servings

Strudel Dough:
Half the quantity of the basic
recipe (p. 14) or 2 store-
bought strudel dough sheets

Filling:
2 cups (300 g) fresh dates*
1 ⅛ cup (100 g) walnuts,
ground
pinch of cinnamon (ground)
1–2 tbsp (2 cl) brandy
about ½ cup (80 g) melted
butter

Coffee Sauce:
See recipe (p. 257)

*Note: Use fresh dates; dried fruits
are too sweet for the strudel.

Prepare homemade strudel dough according to the basic recipe and let rest.

Filling: Peel dates, halve, remove seeds, and mix well with walnuts, cinnamon, and brandy in a bowl.

Stretch out the homemade strudel dough according to the basic recipe. If using store-bought strudel dough: Place two store-bought strudel dough sheets onto a damp cloth so that they overlap slightly, and brush with some melted butter (including the strip of dough located under the "overlap"). Spread filling onto the dough. Roll up the strudel with the help of the cloth, press the outer edges closed, pinch off and cut away excess dough. Using the strudel cloth, place strudel onto a baking sheet lined with parchment paper. Brush with butter and bake in a preheated oven at 400°F (200°C) for about 10 minutes.

Prepare coffee sauce according to the recipe on p. 257.

Remove strudel from oven, brush with remaining butter, cut into approximately ¾ inch pieces, prepare three strudel portions at a time with coffee sauce, and serve sprinkled with powdered sugar. These can be garnished with quartered date pieces.

Pumpkin Strudel with Cinnamon Sauce

Prepare homemade strudel dough according to the basic recipe and let rest

Buttered Bread Crumbs: Melt butter. Brown crumbs in butter together with cinnamon, vanilla sugar, and granulated sugar.

Filling: Peel the pumpkin, scrape out seeds with a tablespoon, coarsely grate the pulp, and mix well with brown sugar, cinnamon, ginger, and vanilla sugar.

Stretch out the homemade strudel dough according to the basic recipe. If using store-bought strudel dough: Place two store-bought strudel dough sheets onto a damp cloth so that they overlap slightly, and brush with some melted butter (including the strip of dough located under the "overlap"). Cut apart a third strudel sheet and place onto the two other sheets so that the area consists of a double layer of dough throughout. Spread butter crumbs on the bottom third. Brush remaining dough area with melted butter. Spread filling onto the butter crumbs and roll up the strudel with the help of the cloth, for homemade strudel dough press the outer edges closed, pinch off and cut away excess dough. Using the strudel cloth, place strudel onto a baking sheet lined with parchment paper. Brush with butter and bake in a preheated oven at 400°F (200°C) for about 30 minutes. Prepare cinnamon sauce according to the recipe (p. 258).

Remove strudel from oven, brush with remaining butter, cut into servings, sprinkle with powdered sugar, and serve with cinnamon sauce.

Yields 10 servings

Strudel Dough:
Basic recipe (p. 14) or 3 store-bought strudel dough sheets

Buttered Bread Crumbs:
½ cup (100 g) butter
2 cups (120 g) bread crumbs
pinch of cinnamon
1 tsp vanilla sugar
1 tbsp granulated sugar

Filling:
2 ¼ lbs (1 kg) pumpkin or squash (best are pumpkins or butternut squash)
1 ¼ cups (150 g) brown sugar
1 tsp cinnamon (ground)
pinch of ginger (ground)
1 tsp vanilla sugar

Cinnamon Sauce:
See recipe (p. 258)

Pears in Strudel Dough

Strudel Dough:
Half the quantity of the basic recipe (p. 14) or 2 store-bought strudel dough sheets about 3 tbsp (40 g) melted butter

5 small pears (e.g., Bartlett)
¾ cup (150 g) granulated sugar
juice of ½ a lemon
¼ cinnamon stick
4 cl (2-3 tbsp) Williams brandy
powdered sugar

Filling:
¾ cup (60 g) almonds, grated, roasted
1 tbsp honey

Raspberry Sauce:
1 ¼ cup (150 g) raspberries
a little over ⅓ cup (50 g) powdered sugar
squeeze of lemon juice

Powdered sugar for sprinkling and raspberries for garnish

Prepare homemade strudel dough according to the basic recipe and let rest.

Wash the pears, peel, and remove stem and core with a corer. In a pot, bring a little over two cups of water to a boil with granulated sugar, lemon juice, cinnamon stick, and Williams brandy. Put in the pears and let soak over low heat until al dente, remove from heat, and let cool in the cooking liquid. **Note:** The pears must be completely covered with liquid.

Remove pears from liquid. Drain four pears and dry well on absorbent paper.

Filling: Mix almonds and honey and fill the pears with it.

Stretch out the homemade strudel dough according to the basic recipe and cut into four equal squares. Halve store-bought strudel dough sheets, place on a damp cloth, and brush with melted butter. Place pears on the strudel sheets and wrap well with strudel dough. Place pears onto a baking sheet lined with parchment paper and bake golden yellow in a preheated oven at 210°C (410°F) for about 8 minutes. Remove pears from the oven, gently cut in half with a serrated knife, and serve on warmed plates with raspberry sauce, sprinkled with powdered sugar and garnished with raspberries.

Raspberry sauce: Wash raspberries, drain well, puree with powdered sugar, press through a sieve, and season to taste with lemon juice.

Variation: Figs also taste very good in strudel dough. Peel the figs, wrap in strudel dough like the pears, and serve with almond or currant sauce.

Topfen-Apricot Strudel with Stewed Apricots

Yields 8 servings

Strudel Dough:
Basic recipe (p. 14), or 3–4 store-bought strudel dough sheets
about ½ cup (100 g) butter

Filling:
½ lb (250 g) apricots
1 ½ cups (350 g) *Topfen* (10% fat)
½ cup (100 g) soft butter
peel of ½ lemon (untreated), zested
1 tsp vanilla sugar
pinch of salt
4 egg yolks
3 egg whites
½ cup (100 g) granulated sugar
2 cups (¼ l) sour cream
½ cup (50 g) flour (fine)
Butter for the mold powdered sugar for sprinkling

Stewed Apricots:
$7/_8$ lb (400 g) apricots
$2/_3$ cup (120 g) granulated sugar
½ cinnamon stick
juice of ½ a lemon
lemon zest (untreated)

If using homemade strudel dough, prepare it according to the basic recipe and let rest. Meanwhile, prepare the filling.

Filling: Wash apricots, core and quarter them, and dry thoroughly on absorbent paper. Press *Topfen* through a sieve with a dough scraper. Stir soft butter, lemon zest, vanilla sugar, and salt until frothy. Gradually stir in *Topfen* and egg yolks. Beat egg whites with granulated sugar until stiff. Stir $1/_3$ of the egg whites with the sour cream into the *Topfen* mix. Finally, fold the remaining egg whites and flour into the mixture.

Stretch out the homemade strudel dough according to the basic recipe, brush with butter, spread on filling, then proceed according to the basic recipe. Place two store-bought strudel dough sheets onto a damp cloth so that they overlap slightly, and brush with some melted butter (including the strip of dough located under the "overlap"). Cut apart a third strudel sheet and place onto the two other sheets so that the area consists of a double layer of dough throughout. Brush with butter. Spread filling onto the bottom third and evenly distribute apricots onto the *Topfen* mixture. Tightly roll up the strudel with the help of the strudel cloth, press strudel ends closed, and cut away excess dough. Using the cloth, place the strudel into a buttered mold, brush with butter and bake in preheated oven at 350°F (180°C) for about 45 minutes. Remove strudel from oven, brush with remaining butter, and let cool for about 15 minutes, cut into servings, sprinkle with powdered sugar, and serve with stewed apricots.

Stewed Apricots: Wash apricots, halve, remove pits, and cut into slices, then bring to a boil with remaining ingredients; cover and let stand for several minutes on low heat. **Note:** Do not overcook the apricots.

Knödel, Pockets, Noodles

Candied fruit was already prevalent in great abundance in the seventeenth and eighteenth centuries, according to cookbooks from that era. *Steckerlobst* (little stick fruit) was the term for the candied grapes, plums, and even nuts that were threaded on wooden sticks. They were a special treat created for the occasion of the Burgundian weddings of the Habsburgers. Glazed fruit could only be found on the tables of princes and of the royal merchants to whom we owe the fact that the precious spices from the Orient are consumer goods today. Sugar, that sweet rarity from India, made the candied fruits expensive, and they could only be obtained in apothecaries. Later on, people experimented with chocolate and marzipan shells, but it took all the way until the *Biedermeier* era for sweet fruit dishes to become a staple in the diet of middle-class households. Inventive housewives tried to substitute loose dough for the expensive chocolate and precious marzipan—and thus the first plum *Knödel* were probably created in place of glazed confections. They were more nutritious and even tastier than the courtly sweets and were quite refined in their own robust fashion. And perhaps it is this kind of country girl charm that proved more popular than the refined enticement of the fruit confections, and why today plum *Knödel* are often offered on menus, but rarely *Steckerlobst*.

Before fruit could become widespread in Austrian cakes and pastries, sugar had to become cheaper. For centuries, fruit played an entirely different role than today. It was eaten steamed and baked with meat dishes, passed out between two main courses, but fruit only began to be discovered as a component of tasty pastries with the democratization of the sweet tooth. Napoleon, the Continental Blockade, and the invention of beet sugar stood at the cradle of fruit pastries.

Fruit *Knödel* as we know them today were probably brought to Vienna more than hundred years ago by Bohemian cooks. Although the *Granatapfel* cookbook from 1699 already included "sour cherry or cherry *Knödel* or *Klößer*," these were not the same as our fruit *Knödel*. They consisted of steamed or boiled fruits which were mixed with bread crumbs roasted in lard and then fried in hot lard.

Only in the mid-nineteenth century could the first plum and apricot *Knödel* made out of potato dough be found in cookbooks, sometimes even with strudel dough.

The origin of the word *Knödel* is the subject of some debate. Whether it comes from the Czech "knedlsk," the Old High German "knoto," or the Middle High German "knode," all of them basically mean hill or knot.

In order for your Knödel to be fragrant, soft, and fluffy, here are some tips:

♦ Shaping *Knödel* must be done by hand! Shape into a compact sphere using both hands and constant pressure. For wet dough—wet hands first with a little lukewarm water, so nothing sticks to your fingers and the *Knödel*'s surface gets nice and smooth. For dry dough—floured hands!

♦ Always place fruit *Knödel* in plenty of lightly salted boiling water, possibly with added sugar, rum, and scraped vanilla bean—then let them soak at low heat with the lid almost closed until done, never let the water come to a full boil, or else the *Knödel* will fall apart.

♦ *Knödel* need room. Only add as many *Knödel* as can float next to one another, as the *Knödel* expand a bit during cooking.

♦ With delicate doughs, possibly cook a test *Knödel*.

♦ Once the *Knödel* float to the surface, they are ready.

♦ For freezing the *Knödel* should be patted dry and while still warm placed individually on plates covered with plastic wrap, then placed in the freezer for about 4 hours of initial freezing before filling into freezer storage bags and kept frozen.

Topfenknödel mit Zwetschkenröster

Topfenteig: Melt butter. Stir *Topfen* with lemon zest, egg, yolk, vanilla sugar, and salt until smooth. Stir in butter, then stir in semolina and chill the mixture for about 1–2 hours.

Stewed Plums: Wash plums, core and quarter them, then bring to a boil with remaining ingredients; cover and stew until soft. Remove cinnamon stick and let the plums cool.

Cut out small portions from the *Topfen* dough with a tablespoon and form *Knödel*. An ice cream scoop is also handy for scooping out small *Knödel* from the *Topfen* dough.

Place *Topfenknödel* in lightly salted boiling water, cover and let stand for about 10 minutes over low heat; return to a boil at the end and cook briefly so that the *Knödel* expand nicely (= souffle-ing).

Buttered Bread Crumbs: Melt butter. Add the bread crumbs and brown until golden, season with cinnamon, vanilla, and granulated sugar to taste.

Remove *Topfenknödel* from the water with a straining ladle and drain well; gently roll in the butter crumbs, sprinkle with powdered sugar, and serve with stewed plums.

The *Topfenknödel* are also delicious with fruit sauces.

Yields 8 servings

Topfenteig:
2 heaping tbsp (30 g) butter
1 cup (250 g) Topfen (20% fat), strained
Peel of ½ lemon (untreated), zested
1 egg
1 egg yolk
1 tsp vanilla sugar
pinch of salt
¼ cup (50 g) wheat semolina

Stewed Plums:
1 ⅓ lbs (600 g) plums
¾ cup (150 g) granulated sugar
juice of ½ lemon
1 cinnamon stick

Buttered Bread Crumbs:
heaping ½ cup (120 g) butter
2 cups (150 g) bread crumbs
pinch of cinnamon (ground)
1 tbsp granulated sugar
1 tsp vanilla sugar

Powdered sugar for sprinkling

Powidltascherln mit Zwetschkenröster

Brandteig:
½ cup (¹/₈ l) milk
1 tbsp butter
salt
¾ cup (80 g) flour (fine)
1 egg yolk
flour for preparing
¹/₃ cup (100 g) *Powidl* (plum jam)
1 egg for brushing

Buttered Bread Crumbs:
3 ½ tbsp (50 g) butter
1 cup (60 g) bread crumbs
pinch of cinnamon
1 tbsp granulated sugar
1 tsp vanilla sugar

Stewed Plums:
Half the quantity of the recipe on p. 261

²/₃ cup (50 g) walnuts, ground, for sprinkling

Brandteig: Bring milk with butter and salt to a boil. Add flour and cook, stirring constantly, until the dough detaches from the bottom of the pot. Transfer dough to a bowl and let cool slightly. Stir yolk into the batter—use an electric mixer for best results. Roll out the dough on a floured surface about ¹/₁₀ of an inch (3 mm) thick, and using a round cookie cutter, cut out circles, then roll out remaining dough again and cut out more pieces until the dough is used up. Put a teaspoonful of *Powidl* jam in the center of each dough circle, brush dough edges with beaten egg. Fold dough over the filling and press dough edges together well (possibly using a fork to compress all around).

Place the pockets in boiling salted water and cook over low heat about 4 minutes.

Buttered Bread Crumbs: Melt butter. Add the bread crumbs and brown until golden, season with cinnamon, vanilla, and granulated sugar to taste.

Remove *Powidl* pockets from the water with a straining ladle and drain well. Gently roll in the butter crumbs and sprinkle with grated walnuts. Serve with stewed plums.

Tip: *Powidl* pockets can also be made from potato dough (p. 40).

Like sorceresses, our grandmothers put fragrant summer and autumn fruits on the table in the middle of winter. Mysterious pots and jars sat waiting in their pantries, containing the harvest of an entire year, such as Powidl plum jam, a sweet treat filling Buchtel and Germknödel. Thank God that nowadays we no longer have to spend hours and hours in an orgy of jam-making for this Bohemian plum jam! Hats off to the housewives of long ago, when there were no preservation factories, no freezers, and no food processors, especially after reading the Original Recipe for Bohemian Zwetschkenlatwerge *(Powidl).*

Strawberry Knödel

Yields 6 servings

Topfenteig:
1 cup (250 g) Topfen (20% fat), strained
¼ cup (60 g) butter, room temperature
peel of ½ lemon (untreated), zested
pinch of salt
1 tsp vanilla sugar
1 egg
1 ½ cups (150 g) flour (fine)
flour for preparing
1 ¹/₃ lb (600 g) strawberries
about
²/₃ cup (100 g) powdered sugar
lemon juice if desired

Buttered Bread Crumbs:
about ½ cup (100 g) butter
2 cups (120 g) bread crumbs
1 pinch of cinnamon
1 tbsp granulated sugar
1 tsp vanilla sugar

Topfenteig: Press *Topfen* through a sieve with a dough scraper. Stir ¼ of the *Topfen* with butter, lemon zest, salt, and vanilla sugar until frothy. Stir in egg, gradually add the remaining *Topfen,* and stir in flour last. Cover and chill *Topfen* dough for about ½ an hour.

Wash and trim strawberries, drain well on absorbent paper. Select 18 nice and firm berries and put them aside for the filling. Puree the remaining strawberries with powdered sugar and season to taste with lemon juice Sprinkle *Topfen* dough lightly with flour and roll it out approximately ¼ inch (½ cm) thick on a floured work surface. Cut out squares from the dough (2 ¾ inch x 2 ¾ inch 7 cm x 7 cm), place one strawberry on each piece, and shape into *Knödel*.

Note: Knead the remaining dough together, chill, roll out again, cut out, and make additional *Knödel*. Place the *Knödel* in boiling salted water and cook over low heat about 7 minutes.

Buttered bread crumbs: Melt butter. Add the bread crumbs and brown until golden, season with cinnamon, vanilla, and granulated sugar to taste.

Remove *Knödel* from the water with a straining ladle, drain well, and roll in the butter crumbs. Sprinkle with powdered sugar and serve with strawberry sauce.

Tip: *Topfen* dough is also wonderfully suited for preparing raspberry and apricot *Knödel*.

Chestnut Knödel

Yields 6 servings

Filling:
7/8 lb (400 g) chestnuts a little
less than
2/3 cup (80 g) powdered sugar
1 tsp vanilla sugar
1–2 tbsp rum

Erdäpfelteig:
7/8 lb (400 g) mealy potatoes
1 cup (100 g) flour (fine)
1 tbsp wheat semolina
pinch of salt
2 heaping tbsp (30 g) butter
1 egg yolk

Flour for preparing

Chocolate sauce:
See recipe (p. 258)
1 cup (100 g) almonds, roasted and grated
1 cup (¼ l) whipping cream

Filling: Cut an X into the chestnuts on the convex side, pour into a pot, cover with water, and cook about 30 minutes until soft (test if done: make sure to peel a chestnut and taste it). Peel chestnuts and press through a sieve. Stir chestnut puree with powdered sugar, vanilla sugar, and rum and chill.

Note: If the mixture gets too hard, add a little powdered sugar.

Erdäpfelteig: Wash potatoes, boil, peel, and let cool for a bit and press through a potato press while still hot. This should yield about ½ lb (250 g) of potato mixture. While still warm, quickly work the mixture into a potato dough with flour, semolina, salt, butter, and egg yolk. Roll out the potato dough on a floured surface about 1/12 inch (2 mm) thick. Cut out pieces from the dough (2 1/3 inches [6 cm] diameter).

Divide the chestnut mixture into three equal portions. Shape two portions into thumb-sized rolls. Put the rest of the chestnut mixture aside for decoration. Cut off 9 pieces from each chestnut roll and place on the dough pieces. Fold dough over the filling and shape into *Knödel* with lightly floured hands.

Place the *Knödel* in boiling salted water and cook over low heat about 10 minutes until done. Press the rest of the chestnut mixture through a grater. Whip cream until stiff.

Remove chestnut *Knödel* from the water with a straining ladle, drain well, and roll in the almonds. Sprinkle chestnut *Knödel* with chestnut puree and serve with chocolate sauce and whipped cream.

Kapuzinerknödel with Coffee Sauce

Kapuzinerknödel: Wash raisins in hot water, drain well, and let dry on absorbent paper. Stir butter with powdered sugar until frothy. Gradually stir in eggs. Mix hazelnuts with the bread crumbs and raisins and stir into the egg mixture. Refrigerate *Knödel* mixture for about 1 hour. Cut out small portions from the mixture with a tablespoon and shape into *Knödel*. Place *Knödel* in hot oil and fry until golden yellow, remove, and drain well. Layer *Knödel* in a buttered heat-resistant casserole dish.

Topping: Whisk the milk with vanilla sugar, pour over the *Knödel*, cover and bake in a preheated oven at 350°F (180°C) **Note:** The *Knödel* are done as soon as the vanilla milk has been completely soaked up.

Coffee Sauce: Stir together vanilla pudding powder with a little coffee and egg yolk. Bring the remaining coffee to a boil with the cream, granulated and vanilla sugars, and salt. Stir in the coffee-yolk mixture and cook, stirring constantly, until the sauce is creamy.

Tip: The sauce may be kept warm over steam. Remove the *Knödel* from the oven and arrange on plates, pour over coffee sauce and serve.

The *Kapuzinerknödel* (Capuchin dumplings) get their name from their resemblance to monkish tonsures.

Yields 8 servings

Kapuzinerknödel:
¼ cup (40 g) raisins
¼ cup (60 g) butter, room temperature
¼ cup (30 g) powdered sugar
pinch of cinnamon (ground)
4 eggs
just under ½ cup (80 g) hazelnuts, grated
1 ¾ cup (100 g) white bread crumbs
16 oz (½ l) oil or fat for frying
butter for the mold

Topping:
½ cup ($^1/_8$ l) milk
1 tsp vanilla sugar

Coffee Sauce:
1 ¼ tbsp (10 g) vanilla pudding powder (or cornstarch)
½ cup ($^1/_8$ l) strong coffee
1 egg yolk
½ cup ($^1/_8$ l) coffee cream (15% fat)
$^1/_3$ cup (70 g) granulated sugar
1 tsp vanilla sugar
pinch of salt

Topfen Noodles in Crumbled Almonds

Yields 4 servings

Topfenteig:
¼ cup (60 g) butter
1 cup (250 g) Topfen (20% fat),
strained peel of ½ lemon (untreated), zested
1 tbsp sour cream
pinch of salt
1 egg
1 egg yolk
$^1/_3$ cup (60 g) wheat semolina
$^1/_3$ cup plus 1 tbsp (40 g) flour (fine) flour for preparing

Strawberry sauce:
½ lb (250 g) strawberries a little over
$^1/_3$ cup (50 g) powdered sugar

Crumbled Almonds:
3 ½ tbsp (50 g) butter
1 cup (100 g) almonds, roasted and grated
1 tsp powdered sugar

Topfenteig: Melt butter. In a bowl, stir *Topfen* together with butter, lemon zest, sour cream, salt, egg, and egg yolk. Mix wheat semolina and flour and stir into the *Topfen* mixture. Cover the *Topfen* dough and chill for about 1–2 hours.

Strawberry sauce: Wash and trim strawberries and drain well. Puree $^2/_3$ of the strawberries with the sugar. Quarter the remaining strawberries and mix in with the puree. Divide dough into two portions and shape each portion into about ¾ inch (2 cm) thick rolls on a floured surface, then cut these into a little over ½ inch (1.5 cm) long pieces with a floured dough scraper and shape them into $^2/_5$ inch (1 cm) thick noodles by hand.

Place the noodles in plenty of boiling salted water and cook over low heat about 5 minutes until done. **Important:** The water shouldn't return to a boil for a few minutes, otherwise the noodles will fall apart!

Crumbled Almonds: Melt butter, stir in almonds with sugar and lightly brown.

Remove noodles from the water with a straining ladle, drain well, and roll in the crumbled almonds. Serve *Topfen* noodles with strawberry sauce.

Note: Before shaping all of the noodles, it's best to cook a "test noodle." If it falls apart or is too hard, fix the consistency of the dough by adding flour or melted butter.

Germknödel

Yields about 15 *Knödel*

1 ¹/₃ tbsp (25 g) fresh yeast
⁷/₈ cup (220 ml) lukewarm milk
4 ½ cups (450 g) flour (fine)
¼ cup (35 g) powdered sugar
1 egg
1 tsp vanilla sugar
just over ¼ cup (55 g) soft butter
peel of ½ lemon (untreated) zested about ²/₃ cup (200 g) *Powidl* (plum jam)
just under ½ tbsp (7 g) salt
flour for preparing
1 egg for brushing salt
about ²/₃ cup (90 g) powdered sugar mixed with 1 ¼ cup (160 g) finely ground poppy seeds
about 1 cup (250 g) hot butter for drizzling

Crumble yeast and dissolve in warm milk (75°F [25°C]). Mix well with about 1 ½ cups (150 g) of flour, sprinkle with flour and let rise in a warm place for about 20 minutes. The volume should double and the surface should show coarse tears. Stir sugar, egg, vanilla sugar, lemon zest, and salt until frothy; mix well with the *Dampfl* and the remaining flour. Knead in the soft butter and let yeast dough rise for 12 minutes.

Knead dough thoroughly once more on a floured work surface with your hands and roll out into a rectangle (about 9.5 inches [24 cm] x 15.75 inches [40 cm]),cut into squares (3 inches [8cm] x 3 inches [8 cm]), put about 1 tsp of *Powidl* on each and brush the dough edges with whisked egg (or water). Shape the dough pieces into *Knödel*. Let the *Knödel* rise with the seam down and covered by a cloth for 20–30 minutes (should about double in volume again), then put on baking paper.

In a large cooking pot, bring plenty of lightly salted water to a boil, put in *Knödel* near the boiling point in several stages and cook with the lid nearly closed over low heat for about 8–10 minutes, turn and cook another 5–8 minutes.

Remove *Germknödel* from the water with a straining ladle, drain well and—important—immediately prick several times with a wooden skewer; in this manner, you prevent your *Knödel* from collapsing. Immediately arrange on plates, sprinkle with poppy seed–powdered sugar mixture, and serve with melted butter.

Topfen Pockets with Stewed Apricots

Yields 6 servings

Topfenteig:
1 cup (250 g) *Topfen* (10% fat)
¼ cup (60 g) butter
peel of ½ lemon (untreated),
zested
1 tbsp sour cream
pinch of rubbed salt
1 egg
1 egg yolk
$^1/_3$ cup (60 g) wheat semolina
$^1/_3$ cup plus 1 tbsp (40 g) flour
(fine) for preparing

Stewed Apricots:
2 ½ heaping cups (400 g)
apricots $^2/_3$ cup (120 g) granulated sugar
3 cl (2 tbsp) apricot brandy
peel and juice of
½ (untreated) lemon zest
½ cinnamon stick

Filling:
½ cup (125 g) Topfen (10%
fat)
1 tbsp melted butter
peel of ½ lemon (untreated),
zested,
¼ cup (30 g) powdered sugar
tsp vanilla sugar
pinch of salt
1 egg yolk
1 tbsp sour cream possibly

1 egg for brushing
½ cup (50 g) almonds, roasted
and grated

Topfenteig: Press *Topfen* through a sieve with a dough scraper. Melt butter. In a bowl, stir *Topfen* together well with butter, lemon zest, sour cream, salt, egg, and egg yolk. Mix semolina and flour and stir into the *Topfen* mixture. Cover *Topfen* dough and let rest in the refrigerator for about 1–2 hours.

Stewed Apricots: Wash apricots, halve, remove pits, and cut into slices. Bring sugar, lemon juice and zest, cinnamon stick, and apricot brandy to a boil. Add apricot slices, cover, and cook over low heat until soft. **Note:** Don't overcook!

Filling: Press *Topfen* through a sieve and stir until smooth with melted butter, lemon zest, powdered and vanilla sugars, salt, egg yolk, and sour cream.

Roll out the *Topfen* dough on a floured surface about $^1/_{10}$ of an inch ($^1/_{10}$ of an inch ([3 mm]) thick. Cut out pieces from the dough (4 inches [10 cm] diameter). Brush dough edges with beaten egg or water and put about 1 tsp filling on each piece of dough. Spread filling with a spoon, leaving the edges free. Fold together dough pieces and press edges closed. Knead remaining dough together again, roll out again, and cut out dough pieces, continuing as before.

Place the *Topfen* pockets in boiling salted water, cover, and cook over low heat about 7 minutes until done. Remove from the water with a straining ladle and drain well.

Sprinkle with grated almonds and serve with stewed apricots.

Apfelnockerln with Cranberries

Apfelnockerln: Wash, peel, and core apples and cut them into small cubes, sprinkle with lemon juice, mix well in a bowl with flour, salt, and yolks and let stand about 15 minutes. Cut out portions from the mixture with a tablespoon, shape *Nockerln* with floured hands, and place them in boiling salted water.* Cover and cook over low heat about 8 minutes until done.

Note: The water must not be at a rolling boil, otherwise the *Nockerln* will fall apart!

Remove from the water with a straining ladle and drain well. In the meantime, mix granulated sugar with cinnamon.

Sprinkle *Nockerln* with cinnamon sugar and serve with cranberry sauce.

---

* It is a good idea to put a test *Nockerl* in the salted water before cooking all of the *Nockerln*. If this *Nockerl* falls apart, add a little flour to the dough.

Yields 6 servings

Apfelnockerln:
a little over 1 lb (½ kg) apples
(preferably Golden Delicious)
lemon juice
3 tbsp flour (fine)
2 egg yolks
pinch of salt
flour for preparing

½ cup minus
1 tbsp (80 g) granulated sugar
1 pinch of cinnamon (ground)

Cranberry Sauce:
See recipe (p. 258) or ready-made cranberry sauce.

Grießknödel

Yields about 10 servings

2 ½ cups (600 g) milk
2 heaping tbsp (30 g) butter
just under 2 tbsp (15 g) vanilla
sugar
¾ heaping tbsp (12 g) salt
1 ¼ cup (210 g) wheat
semolina
2 eggs

**Poppy Seed-Almond Bread
Crumbs:**

1 ⅛ cup (150 g) poppy seeds,
finely ground 1 ½ cups (150
g) (or hazelnuts),
roasted and grated heaping ⅔
cup (100 g) powdered sugar

Raspberry Sauce:
3 ¼ cup (400 g) raspberries
(can be frozen)
½ cup (100 g) granulated
sugar

Bring milk to a boil with butter, vanilla sugar, and ⅔ tbsp (10 g) salt, add semolina while constantly stirring and let swell. Let cool slightly. Stir in eggs.

Shape *Knödel* from the mixture with moistened hands. Place the *Knödel* in boiling, slightly salted water and cook over low heat about 10 minutes with an almost closed lid.

Poppy Seed-Almond Bread Crumbs: Mix poppy seeds with almonds, powdered and vanilla sugars.

Raspberry Sauce: Mix raspberries with granulated sugar and strain.

Remove *Knödel* from the water with a straining ladle, drain well, and roll in the poppy seeds/crumbled almonds. Serve with raspberry sauce.

Poppy Seed Noodles

Yields 4 servings

Erdäpfelteig:
See recipe (p. 40)
a little over $1/_3$ cup (50 g)
ground poppy seeds
a little over $1/_3$ cup (50 g)
powdered sugar
1 tbsp butter

Prepare potato dough according to the recipe. Shape dough on a floured work surface into two thumb-sized rolls, cut these into a little over ½ inch (1.5 cm) long pieces with a floured dough scraper, and shape them into $2/_5$ inch (1 cm) thick noodles by hand. Place the noodles in boiling salted water, cover, and cook over low heat about 5 minutes.*

Note: The water shouldn't return to a boil for a few minutes, otherwise the noodles will fall apart! Carefully remove from the water with a straining ladle and drain well.

In the meantime, roast poppy seeds with powdered sugar in butter. Roll the noodles in this, and serve with powdered sugar.

Tip: Browned butter can also be dripped on the poppy seed noodles.

*It is a good idea to cook a test noodle before shaping all of the noodles. If it falls apart or is too hard, fix the consistency of the dough by working in flour or melted butter.

Waldviertler Plum Knödel

Sauce: Wash and trim plums. Core, quarter, and cut $7/_8$ cup (150 g) of plums into large pieces. Bring plum pieces to a boil with ¼ cup ($1/_{16}$ l) water, sugar, cinnamon stick, and slivovitz; stew plums to a thick stew, remove cinnamon stick, puree plum stew with hand blender, and chill.

Filling: Wash plums, core using a wooden spoon, and fill each with one cube of sugar.

Erdäpfelteig: Prepare dough as described on p. 40. Roll out dough $1/_5$ inch (½ cm) thick on a floured work surface. Cut out 12 pieces from the dough (3 inches [8 cm] diameter). Put one plum on each piece of dough and shape into *Knödel* with floured hands. Place the *Knödel* in boiling salted water, cover, and cook over low heat about 10 minutes. Remove *Knödel* from the water with a straining ladle and drain well. In the meantime, mix poppy seeds and powdered sugar. Arrange dumplings on a plate with plum sauce, sprinkle with poppy seed sugar, and serve.

Tip: Brandteig (see recipe, p. 120) is also suitable for plum dumplings.

Yields 4–6 servings

Plum Sauce:
$7/_8$ lb (400 g) plums
a little less than ½ cup (90 g) granulated sugar
juice of ½ lemon
1 cinnamon stick

Filling:
12 plums
12 cubes of sugar

Erdäpfelteig:
See recipe (p. 40)
flour for preparing
salt a little over
$1/_3$ cup (50 g) gray poppy seeds, finely ground
¾ cup (30 g) powdered sugar

Auflauf, Pudding, Wiener Koch, and Soufflé

"Since ancient times, the Auflauf [casserole dish] has been known, appreciated, and respected here, its costliness the only obstacle to becoming as common among the lower classes as the *Knödel*." Thus reads a description from the kitchen literature of the eighteenth century on the distinctiveness of the *Auflauf*.

The *Koch* is a typical Austrian specialty that can be found in two different versions in our kitchens: in rural areas, certain fat-rich, porridge-like dishes made from flour or semolina were known as—and are sometimes still known as—a *Koch*. Thus, for example, the *Almkoch* (Alpine), *Schmalzkoch* (lard), and *Taufkoch* (baptismal) were all well established as traditional and festive dishes. In the *Bucklige Welt* region of southeastern Lower Austria, a common ancient custom was to eat no less than nine different *Koch*s the night before Epiphany—and to leave the leftovers at the dining table for the Three Wise Men.

In contrast, the *Wiener Koch* (Viennese) is—as the name suggests—a creation of the Viennese pastry kitchen. The base of the *Wiener Koch* is either sliced bread rolls or croissants (reusing leftovers!), which are mixed with eggs, milk, and flavorings and baked in a pan in the oven. Or it can also be made from sponge cake, which can also have nuts, almonds, or chocolate added and which is also baked in the oven.

The exact boundary between an *Auflauf* and a *Koch* is impossible to find, since the *Auflauf* was probably developed out of the *Wiener Koch*. The *Koch* was refined by folding egg whites into the base, and this "risen *Koch*" later became known as an "*Auflauf*." Ultimately this dish made its way to Paris by accident and was modified by the chefs there. Through this refinement process, what had been a dish made from leftovers became an exquisite casserole in the nineteenth century, while at the same time becoming very popular: The well-known gastrosopher Brillat-Savarin called it "that certain dot on the 'i'" of a menu, whereupon it soon became popular in many countries.

Soufflé was the term for those casseroles that rose especially high during baking due to the addition of large amounts of egg whites—meant to be brought straight from the oven to the table so that the laboriously worked in air didn't escape again and the culinary work of art didn't collapse. The *soufflés*, also known as "*Schaumauflauf*" (cream casserole) are among the lightest dishes because of their consistency, but also among the trickiest. The most essential element of the *soufflé* is the egg white, which is predominantly responsible for success or failure of the dish: The air that is beaten into the egg whites expands during baking, allowing the *soufflé*—when properly prepared—to rise and be loose and fluffy. **Important:** Both the container and the whisk must be completely clean and free of grease, as the slightest contamination will prevent the egg whites from stiffening.

The base of an *Auflauf* is usually cooked—such as the rice, semolina, or noodle *Auflauf*—but can also be prepared "cold," such as the nut *Auflauf*.

*Koch*s cooked in a water bath—usually in individual portion molds—are known as *Dunstkochs* (steam) or puddings (e.g., *Mohr im Hemd*, literally "Moor in a Shirt," a type of chocolate pudding). **Important:** Only fill molds ¾ of the way with the base so that the *Dunstkoch* can rise well during cooking.

Poaching in a water bath: With this method of cooking, puddings and *Dunstkochs* turn out particularly soft and fluffy and cannot burn.

Variation 1: Poaching in the oven: Preheat oven to 350°F (180°C). Coat ramekins with butter and sprinkle with sugar. Prepare pudding base according to recipe. Meanwhile, put on water for the water bath. Place the molds/ramekins in a roasting pan or baking dish and pour in enough boiling water to halfway submerge the ramekins in the water bath. Cook puddings in the preheated oven.

Variation 2: Poaching on the stove: Place a few layers of baking paper on the bottom of a sufficiently large pot (to prevent slipping), add filled molds, pour hot water into the pot so that the ramekins are halfway submerged in the water bath. Cover the pot except for a crack and cook the puddings on low heat (water should not boil!).

Drunken Kapuziner

Kapuziner: Stir together eggs with granulated and vanilla sugars, salt, cinnamon, and lemon zest in a mixing bowl and beat over steam until thick and creamy. Remove from heat and keep beating it—preferably over ice water—until it cools to room temperature ("beating cold"). Then fold in almonds and flour to the mixture. Pour mixture into buttered and floured small molds (each about ½ cup [¹/₈ l]) and bake in preheated oven at 350°F (180°C) for about 25 minutes. Place *Kapuziner* upside down on a pan sprinkled with granulated sugar and let cool in their molds.

Broth: Bring pineapple juice to a boil with sugar, 2 tbsp water, white wine, and rum.

Turn *Kapuziner* over in their molds and set upright; douse with the hot liquid (all of the liquid should be absorbed). Turn the drunken *Kapuziners* out of the molds on to a plate and serve with whipped cream.

Note: Drunken *Kapuziners* also taste delicious chilled.

Yields 10 servings

Kapuziner:
4 eggs
¾ heaping cup (160 g) granulated sugar
1 tsp vanilla sugar
pinch of salt
pinch of ground cinnamon
peel of ½ lemon (untreated), zested
1 cup (80 g) almonds or hazelnuts, grated
1 ¹/₃ cup plus
1 tbsp (140 g) flour (fine)

Butter and flour for the pans
Granulated sugar

For Soaking:
¹/₃ cup (80 ml) pineapple juice (canned)
¹/₃ cup (60 g) granulated sugar
½ cup (¹/₃ l) white wine
1 shot of rum
1 cup (¼ l) whipping cream

Rice Auflauf with Apples

Auflauf:
about $^7/_8$ cup (180 g)
short grain rice
2 ¾ cup (650 ml) milk
¼ cup (60 g) butter
pinch of salt
2 tsp vanilla sugar
peel of ½ lemon (untreated),
zested
6 eggs
½ cup minus
1 tbsp (80 g) granulated sugar
butter and bread crumbs for
the pan

Caramelized Apples:
a little over 1 lb (½ kg) apples
(such as Golden Delicious, Jona
Gold)
3 ½ tbsp (50 g) butter or
clarified butter
3 tbsp granulated sugar

Powdered sugar for sprinkling

Blanch rice in a little over 2 cups (½ l) of water for 3 minutes, strain, rinse cold, and drain well. Bring milk to a boil with butter, salt, 1 tsp vanilla sugar, and lemon zest, add rice and cook until soft over low heat for about 20 minutes. Let cool. Separate eggs. Stir yolks with remaining vanilla sugar until frothy and stir in rice mixture. Beat egg whites with granulated sugar until stiff and fold in. Fill rice mixture into a buttered casserole dish sprinkled with bread crumbs and smooth. Bake rice casserole in a preheated oven at 310°F (160°C) for about 1 hour.

Caramelized Apples: Peel apples, core, and cut into slices. Melt some butter in a pan, briefly roast apples in it, and remove from pan. Lightly caramelize granulated sugar with the remaining butter in the pan; briefly toss apple slices in it.

Remove rice *Auflauf* from the oven and let rest for about 5 minutes; divide into portions while still warm, sprinkle with powdered sugar, and serve. Serve with apples.

Testing if Done: Stick a kitchen needle into the rice *Auflauf*. If the needle stays clean, the rice *Auflauf* is ready.

Scheiterhaufen with Schneehaube

Yields 10 servings
(as dessert)

Filling:
just under1 lb (400 g) apples
(such as Cox Orange, Jona Gold)
about ½ cup ($^1/_8$ l) white wine
3 tbsp granulated sugar
½ cinnamon stick
$^1/_3$ cup (50 g)raisins

Scheiterhaufen:
12 oz (350 g) milk loaf, Striezel
(Austrian plaited bun), brioche,
or white bread
3 eggs
peel of ½ lemon (untreated),
zested
1 ½ cup (350 ml) milk
pinch of salt
1 tsp vanilla sugar
$^1/_3$ cup (60 g) granulated sugar
3 ½ tbsp (50 g) ghee or clarified butter*
approximately 3 ½ tbsp (50 g)
butter and
½ cup (30 g) bread crumbs for
the mold

Schneehaube:
3 egg whites
¾ cup (140 g) granulated sugar
powdered sugar for sprinkling

Raspberry Sauce:
3 ¼ cup (400 g) raspberries
(frozen)
heaping $^2/_3$ cup (100 g) powdered sugar
*Clarified butter: Melt butter, heat,
and skim foam from the surface.

Wash apples, peel, core, and cut into thin slices. Bring white wine to a boil with sugar and cinnamon, insert apples, and poach over low heat. Remove apples from the liquid with a straining ladle and drain well. Wash raisins in hot water and drain well on absorbent paper.

Remove crusts from milk loaf and cut in about $^1/_5$ inch (½ cm) thick slices; place in a bowl. Separate eggs. Stir yolks with lemon zest, milk, salt, and vanilla sugar and pour over milk loaf slices. Let stand for about 10 minutes. Beat egg whites with half the amount of sugar until stiff, add remaining sugar, and beat until stiff peaks form. Carefully mix egg whites into the bread mixture. Fill half the mixture into a buttered dish sprinkled with bread crumbs, smooth the surface, distribute apple slices evenly on top, sprinkle with raisins, and pour remaining mixture onto the apples. Heat the ghee or clarified butter and sprinkle onto the *Scheiterhaufen*; bake in a preheated oven at 325°F (170°C) for about 1 hour. Take *Scheiterhaufen* out of the oven.

Schneehaube: Beat egg whites with sugar warm over steam (104–113°F or 40–45°C), remove from heat and then beat cold (continue beating until the egg whites are "stable"). Spread $^1/_3$ of the *Schnee* onto the *Scheiterhaufen*. Fill remaining egg whites into a pastry bag with a serrated tip and decorate the *Schnee* with it; sprinkle with powdered sugar and bake in the oven at 500°F (250°C) until the *Schnee* is lightly browned (doesn't take long!). Cut *Scheiterhaufen* out of the dish in portions and serve with raspberry sauce.

Raspberry Sauce: Puree raspberries with sugar, strain through a sieve.

The *Scheiterhaufen* with *Schneehaube* is a very descriptive term for the visual appearance of this dish: the *Scheiterhaufen* was the stake where heretics or witches were burnt, and *Schneehaube* literally means "Snow Cover."

Salzburger Nockerln with Currant Sauce

Yields 4 servings

Nockerl Mixture:
just under ½ cup (100 g) whipping cream
1 ½ tbsp (20 g) butter
3 egg yolks
just under ¼ cup (20 g) flour (fine)
peel of ½ lemon (untreated), zested 5 egg whites
3 $\frac{1}{3}$ tbsp (40 g) granulated sugar
1 tsp vanilla sugar

Currant Sauce:
1 $\frac{1}{3}$ cup (150 g) currants
½ cup minus 1 tbsp (80 g) granulated sugar
2 cl (1 tbsp) currant liqueur

Powdered sugar for sprinkling

First, prepare the currant sauce: Wash currants, pluck from the stems, and drain well. Bring $\frac{2}{3}$ of the currants to a boil with 4 tbsp water and sugar, puree briefly. (**Note:** the currant seeds should stay whole, otherwise the sauce will be bitter). Strain currant puree through a sieve and flavor with liqueur. Mix in remaining currants, bring sauce to a boil again, and let cool.

Salzburger Nockerln: Pour whipping cream into a heat-resistant pan, add butter, and place the pan into preheated oven. Meanwhile quickly stir together yolks with flour and lemon zest. **Note:** If the mixture is too solid, add a few drops of water. Beat egg whites with granulated and vanilla sugars until stiff, stir $\frac{1}{3}$ of egg whites into the yolk mixture. "Lightly" fold in remaining egg whites.

Using a large spoon or a dough scraper, shape *Nockerln* from the *Nockerl* mixture, place in the heated pan, and bake for about 6 minutes in a preheated oven at 425°F (220°C). *Salzburger Nockerln* should be gently browned on the surface and the interior should still be creamy.

Sprinkle *Salzburger Nockerln* with powdered sugar and serve with currant sauce. These also taste excellent with vanilla sauce or cranberry sauce!

Salzburger Nockerln: This world-famous dessert, part of the soufflé family, was supposedly first prepared for the Salzburg archbishop Wolf Dietrich.

Topfen Auflauf with Strawberries

Yields 6 to 8 servings

1 cup (250 g) Topfen (10% fat)
3 eggs
1 tsp vanilla sugar
peel of ½ lemon (untreated),
zested
½ cup (¹/₈ l) sour cream
1 tsp cornstarch
pinch of salt
3 ¹/₃ tbsp (40 g) granulated
sugar
butter and granulated sugar for
the dishes

Strawberry Sauce:
²/₃ cup (100 g) of the recipe
(p. 262)

Press *Topfen* through a sieve with a dough scraper. Separate eggs.

Stir *Topfen* with yolks, lemon zest, sour cream, cornstarch, and salt until smooth. Beat egg whites with sugar until stiff and fold into the *Topfen* mixture with a whisk.

Fill *Topfen* mixture ¾ of the way into buttered dishes sprinkled with granulated sugar (about ½ cup [¹/₈ l] content). Fill a heat-resistant dish about ²/₅ inch (1 cm) high with water and bring water to a boil. Put in the dishes and cook in a preheated oven at 400°F (200°C) (**Note:** only lower heat!) for 20 minutes. Turn out the *Topfen Auflauf* onto a plate.

Serve with strawberry sauce and fresh strawberries.

Cinnamon Auflauf with Poached Pears

Poached Pears: Wash pears, peel, halve, and remove cores with a small spoon. Bring ½ cup (¹/₈ l) water to a boil with sugar, lemon juice, red wine, cassis, and cinnamon stick. Put in pears, boil, and let stand over low heat until they are soft (**Note:** They shouldn't be so soft that they fall apart). Remove pears from the broth with a straining ladle and drain it off. Pour half the amount of the broth back over the pears. Stir cornstarch with a little cold water until smooth. Bring remaining broth to a boil, stir in cornstarch, and simmer the broth to a creamy consistency. Refrigerate cream.

Cinnamon Auflauf: Melt Couverture chocolate coating over steam (maximum 104°F [40°C]). Separate eggs. Stir butter with vanilla sugar, cinnamon, and salt until frothy. Gradually stir yolk and liqueur into the butter mixture. Fold in molten chocolate. Mix almonds with flour. Beat egg whites with granulated sugar until soft peaks form and stir in to the chocolate-cinnamon mixture together with the almond flour using a whisk.

Pour mixture into buttered pans sprinkled with granulated sugar (about ½ cup [¹/₈ l] content). Lay paper in a heat resistant dish (so that the molds don't slip so easily), fill about ²/₅ inch (1 cm) high with water and bring water to a boil. Place molds inside and bake for about 40 minutes in a preheated oven at 400°F (200°C). Remove pears from the red wine broth, cut in slices, and arrange in a fan shape on a plate. Pour over cream. Carefully turn out cinnamon soufflés on top, sprinkle with powdered sugar, and serve immediately.

Yields 6 servings

Cinnamon Auflauf:
2 ounces (60 g) dark Couverture chocolate coating
3 eggs
¼ cup (60 g) butter at room temperature
1 tsp vanilla sugar
1 level tsp cinnamon (ground)
Pinch of salt
¹/₃ cup (60 g) granulated sugar
2 cl (1–2 tbsp) brandy
¾ cup (60 g) almonds, grated
2 tbsp flour (fine)

Butter and granulated sugar for the dishes
powdered sugar for sprinkling

Poached Pears:
3 pears
(e.g., Bartlett)
²/₃ cup (120 g) granulated sugar
juice of 2 lemons
1 cup (¼ l) red wine
4 cl cassis (currant liqueur)
½ cinnamon stick
2 tsp cornstarch

Wine Soufflé

2 ¾ tbsp (40 g) butter
$^1/_3$ cup plus 1 tbsp (40 g) flour
(fine)
½ cup ($^1/_8$ l) white wine
pinch of salt
peel of ½ lemon (untreated),
zested
4 eggs
2 egg whites
½ cup (100 g) granulated
sugar

Butter and granulated sugar
for the molds
powdered sugar for sprinkling

Melt butter, stir in flour; while stirring gradually, pour the wine into the light roux, add salt and lemon zest, bring to a boil, and stir vigorously, remove from heat, and let cool slightly. Separate eggs. Stir yolks into the mixture. Beat 6 egg whites with granulated sugar until soft peaks form and carefully add to the mixture.

Fill soufflé mixture ¾ of the way into four buttered molds sprinkled with granulated sugar (about ½ cup [$^1/_8$ l] content with flat bottoms).

Fill a large ovenproof pan about $^2/_5$ inch (1 cm) high with water, bring to a boil, and bake the soufflé in a water bath in a preheated oven at 410°F (210°C) lower heat for about 20 minutes. Remove soufflés from the oven, sprinkle with sugar, and serve.

Tip: These go very well with currant sauce or wine sauce.

Mohr im Hemd

Yields 6 servings

Mohr im Hemd:
½ cup (50 g) chocolate
3 ½ tbsp (50 g) softened butter
1 tsp vanilla sugar
pinch of salt
3 eggs
about ⅓ cup (50 g) ground hazelnuts,
¼ cup (50 g) granulated sugar
1 tbsp bread crumbs
Butter and granulated sugar for the molds

Chocolate Sauce:
See recipe (p. 258)
1 cup (¼ l) whipping cream
1 tsp vanilla sugar chocolate shavings for garnish

Melt chocolate over steam (maximum 104°F [40°C]). Stir soft butter, vanilla sugar, and salt until frothy. Separate eggs. Gradually mix yolks in with the butter mixture, fold in chocolate. Beat egg whites with granulated sugar until soft peaks form. Stir egg whites, hazelnuts, and bread crumbs into the chocolate mixture with a whisk.

Fill the mixture about ¾ of the way up in small buttered molds sprinkled with granulated sugar. Pour about ⅖ inch (1 cm) of water into a correspondingly large heat-resistant pan, bring to a boil, and put in the molds. Bake in preheated oven at 400°F (200°C) for about 40 minutes.

Chocolate sauce: Prepare according to the recipe on p. 258.

Beat whipping cream with vanilla sugar until stiff. Take puddings out of the oven, turn out of the molds onto plates, and decorate with chocolate sauce, whipped cream, and chocolate shavings.

Tip: So that the molds don't slip in the pan, place parchment paper on the bottom of the pan and place the molds on it.

Semolina Pudding with Applesauce

Yields 8 servings

Semolina Pudding:
a little over 1 ½ cups
(³/₈ l) milk
2 ¾ tbsp (40 g) butter
1 tsp vanilla sugar
pinch of salt
peel of ½ lemon (untreated),
zested
just under ½ cup (80 g) wheat
semolina
5 eggs
¼ cup (50 g) granulated sugar
butter and granulated sugar for
the molds

Applesauce:
See recipe (p. 256)

Semolina Pudding: Bring milk, butter, vanilla sugar, salt, and lemon zest to a boil. Add semolina while stirring and bring to a boil while constantly stirring; let cool. Separate eggs. Stir yolk with 1 tbsp of granulated sugar until frothy. Beat egg whites with remaining granulated sugar until stiff. Stir yolk mixture into the semolina mixture, and then fold in egg whites.

Fill the semolina mixture about ¾ of the way up in small buttered molds sprinkled with granulated sugar (about ½ cup [¹/₈ l] each). Fill a heat-resistant pan about ²/₅ inch (1 cm) high with water and bring water to a boil. Place molds inside and bake for about 30 minutes in a preheated oven at 400°F (200°C).

Applesauce: Prepare according to the recipe on p. 256.

Poppy Seed Pudding (Mohnkoch)

Yields 6-8 servings

Poppy Seed Pudding:
2 ¾ cups (100 g) white bread
1 tbsp rum
⁷/₈ cup (200 ml) milk
¹/₃ cup (80 g) butter at room
temperature
pinch of salt
1 pinch of ground cinnamon
1 tsp vanilla sugar
4 eggs
½ cup minus 1 tbsp (80 g)
granulated sugar
²/₃ cup (90 g) ground poppy
seeds
1 tbsp bread crumbs butter,
sugar for the molds

Raspberry Sauce:
See recipe (p. 256)

Almond sauce:
See recipe (p. 257)

Poppy Seed Pudding: Remove crusts from white bread, cut into small cubes, and sprinkle with rum. Boil milk and pour over the bread cubes, let stand for about 10 minutes. Then puree (blender or hand blender) or press through a sieve and chill. Stir together butter, salt, cinnamon, and vanilla sugar until creamy. Separate eggs. Gradually stir yolk and white bread puree stir into the butter. Beat egg whites with granulated sugar until soft peaks form. Fold egg whites, poppy seeds, and breadcrumbs with a whisk fold into the mixture. Fill the poppy seed mixture about ¾ of the way up in small buttered molds sprinkled with sugar (about ½ cup [¹/₈ l] each).

Fill a heat-resistant mold about 1 inch high with water and bring water to a boil. Place molds inside and bake for about 35 minutes in a preheated oven at 400°F (200°C).

In the meantime, prepare raspberry and almond sauces according to the recipe.

Turn poppy seed pudding out onto plates and decorate with raspberry and almond sauce.

Chestnut Pudding

Chestnut Pudding: Melt chocolate over steam (max. 104°F [40°C]). Stir soft butter with vanilla sugar and salt until frothy. Separate eggs. Stir yolk and chestnut puree into the butter mixture. Fold in chocolate. Beat egg whites with granulated sugar until soft peaks form and alternately fold in with the almonds. Fill the chestnut mixture about ¾ of the way up in small buttered molds sprinkled with sugar (about ½ cup [1/8 l] each). Fill a heat-resistant mold about 1 inch high with water and bring water to a boil. Place molds inside and bake for about 30 minutes in a preheated oven at 400°F (200°C).

Chocolate sauce: Bring whipping cream to a boil, coarsely chop both couvertures, stir in, and let melt. Briefly blend chocolate sauce with a hand blender. Whip cream until stiff. Turn out chestnut pudding onto plates, drizzle with half of the chocolate sauce, decorate with whipped cream and serve.

Yields 8 servings

Chestnut Pudding:
$1/_3$ cup (30 g) dark chocolate couverture
just under 5 tbsp (70 g) butter at room temperature
1 tsp vanilla sugar
pinch of salt
3 eggs
about ½ cup (60 g) chestnut puree*
$1/_3$ cup (60 g) granulated sugar
¾ cup (60 g) almonds, roasted and ground
Butter and granulated sugar for the molds

Chocolate Sauce:
a little over 1 cup (250 ml) whipping cream
a little over ¾ cup (80 g) milk chocolate couverture
1 ¼ cup (120 g) dark chocolate couverture

1 cup (¼ l) whipping cream for decorating

*Chestnut puree: Fresh chestnut puree tastes better and more intensively than store-bought. Cut an X into the chestnuts on the curved side, cook in plenty of water for about 30 minutes, drain, peel, and press through a sieve.

Schmarren, Omelets, Palatschinken, Dalken, and more

Schmarren was basically a rural, peasant dish and in its original form is more like a hearty *Sterz* (a traditional rural dish similar to polenta made from cereals). A "fat *Schmarren*" is first mentioned in 1563 in the wedding sermon of the German pastor Johannes Mathesius, underscoring that the etymological root of *Schmarren* is *Schmer*—meaning lard or fat. *Schmarren* was in fact a hearty meal that was mainly prepared by woodcutters or dairymen on open fires to give them strength for a long day of work.

It didn't become "presentable" in bourgeois urban households until whipped egg whites were added to the *Schmarren* for fluffy lightness, raisins and sugar for tempting sweetness, and butter for its melting delicacy. Eighteenth-century cookbooks already contained the *Schmarren* recipes known today such as *Mehl-Schmarn* (flour *Schmarren*), *Griess-Schmarrn* (semolina *Schmarren*), and *Semmel-Schmarn* (bread *Schmarren*). The "*Grätzerische Kochbuch*" also contains a *Reisschmarn* (rice *Schmarren*); in 1827 Anna Dorn includes ordinary *Mehl-schmarren* and *Semmelschmarren*, Rokitansky adds cherry, sponge cake, apple, and *Topfen Schmarren* and the *Gaadner Schmarren* to the *Schmarren* repertory.

Franz Zelena (1828) refined the *Schmarren* by using cream instead of milk, increasing the number of eggs, and also says: "The sugar can be mixed with any of the aromas of vanilla, orange or cinnamon."

Around 1850 this version is first described as *Kaiserschmarren*—maybe as a tribute to the young emperor Franz Joseph, but just like the many "*Schmarren* legends," this cannot be proven. The most popular story is of Leopold, the imperial couple's personal chef, who wanted to gain favor with the empress. She was watching her weight but still had a sweet tooth, and so he came up with a new creation of shredded pancake dough and stewed plums. But the dish was supposedly left untouched, whereupon the Kaiser ate up the whole thing with the words "Well, pass down that rubbish [*Schmarren* is Austrian slang for rubbish or nonsense to this day] that our Poldl has thrown together this time."

Another anecdote tells of an imperial hunt that ended at a dairyman's (in Austria also known as a *Käser* [cheeser]), who served the Kaiser a *Käserschmarren*—the Kaiser is said to have been so enthusiastic that he renamed the dish "*Kaiserschmarren.*"

However, certainly some indications point to the *Kaiserschmarren* being from the Southern Alps, where it was called *Casa Schmarren*, i.e., house *Schmarren*, and was subsequently elevated to *Kaiserschmarren*.

Tips:
- Use as large a frying pan as possible for preparing the *Kaiserschmarren*.
- Melt the butter in it, add about ¾ of an inch (2 cm) of batter, and commence cooking on low heat until the underside is lightly browned. **Careful:** Due to the sugar content, the *Kaiserschmarren* turns brown very quickly. Sprinkle with (rum-soaked) raisins.
- Separate the *Schmarren* in the center with a spatula or plastic dough scraper and carefully flip each half using the spatula. **Note:** The less you cut the *Schmarren* before flipping, the fluffier it becomes.
- After flipping, finish baking the *Schmarren* in the oven, then cut it into small, irregular pieces using two forks.
- Finally, add a little more butter, sprinkle the *Schmarren* with a little sugar, let it caramelize, and bake the *Schmarren* until each piece of *Schmarren* is crispy on the outside.
- Most *Schmarrens* can be wonderfully prepared in advance. In order to prepare, mix all of the ingredients well except the beaten egg whites, and then once the guests arrive, fold in the egg whites and bake the *Schmarren*.

One should most definitely follow the advice given to his readers by F. G. Zenker in the book *The Artful Bakery* : "It is better for the guests to wait on the *Schmarren* than the *Schmarren* on the guests."

Palatschinken are certainly one of the most precious heirlooms of the monarchist cuisine. In Hungarian, they are called "*Palacsinta*"; in Czech, "*Palacinka.*" The most luxurious variants come from there, the *Gundelpalatschinken* enriched with tipsy nut filling, chocolate sauce, and whipped cream, the Bohemian *Palatschinken* filled with *Topfen* cream, stacked like roof tiles, and baked in layers with cream and eggs, or the Hungarian *Gleitpalatschinken* served with fragrant punch cream. In contrast, the classic apricot *Palatschinke* is practically a meal for ascetics.

Palatschinken are cosmopolitan and rather ancient; one of mankind's oldest meals is flat bread toasted on hot stones, the original form of bread. In ancient Transylvania, there was a custom of baking flat breads made out of yeast dough on hot bricks. From there, the dish arrived in Hungary and then to Slovenia. The *Palatschinken* ultimately became part of

Austrian pastry cuisine via the detour of Bohemian cooking. The Viennese *Palatschinke* first established itself in the nineteenth century. In old cookbooks, only pancakes (in Austrian variously called *Pfannkuchen, Pfannzelten, Eierkuchen, Omeletten,* or *Dalken*) are mentioned.

Today the Viennese distinguish precisely between the different designations. *Palatschinken* are made from a runny batter and are smaller. A *Pfannkuchen*—today this term is common especially in Germany—is made of a thickish *Palatschinken* batter. The *Omelette* is the refined stage of *Pfannkuchen* and *Palatschinke* and was a very popular dish especially in the eighteenth century. In old cookbooks, the *Omelette* is known as the Spanish *Strudelfleck.*

Even today, baked flat breads are a staple in many cultures: "*Tortillas*" in Mexico, "*Chapati*" in India, in France the "*Crepes*", paper-thin "*Crespelle*" in Italy, "*Dorati*" in Switzerland. Whether *Crepes, Crespelle,* or *Palatschinken,* in their present form they are the missing link between ancient foodstuffs and modern delights for the taste buds, one that has entered finer cuisine as well.

In order for Palatschinken to become paper-thin, there are a few tricks:
- First, you should specifically reserve a pan in which nothing else will be cooked but *Palatschinken*. A coated pan is good since the batter should never swim in grease. Even better is an iron pan. However, these must first be "burned out" before using. This involves sprinkling a handful of salt into the pan and heating it until it's very hot. Thereafter, the pan is wiped off with a paper towel and from then on never washed again, but instead only wiped clean with a paper towel after each *Palatschinken* session. *Palatschinken* will namely stick to a pan that has been treated with detergent, which is why in old cookbooks you can find mentioned: "A cook that's too clean isn't good for the *Palatschinken!*"
- **Batter:** The basic ingredients are always the same: flour, milk, and eggs. All other ingredients are used for refinement: If part of the milk is replaced by cream, then the *Palatschinken* turn out particularly rich. Carbonated mineral water loosens the batter. Adding fat (clarified butter) makes the dough very tender.
- The thinner the batter, the thinner the *Palatschinken*. If it is too thin, the *Palatschinken* will tear when turning. Exact amounts cannot be given; it depends on the gluten and moisture content of the flour and the size of the eggs.
- In order for the batter to be nice and smooth, it is best to mix it with a hand blender, or to strain it through a sieve.
- Always let the batter rest for at least 10 minutes.
- **Cooking Fat:** Heat a little butter or clarified butter, the fat should be hot, but not allowed to smoke! Make sure the pan is very hot before heating the fat in it. Best is to brush out the pan with a greased brush—the pan should only be coated with a thin coat of grease.
- Pour in the batter and distribute evenly by tilting the pan. Pour off excess batter from the pan. Cook *Palatschinken* until the underside is lightly browned, and then first loosen the *Palatschinken* at the edges using a spatula or plastic dough scraper before flipping it with momentum and cooking it until light brown on the other side. If the *Palatschinken* are cooked too hot, holes will result.

Dalken are among the pastry desserts of Bohemian and, to some extent, Slavic origin. Already in the fourteenth century, the *Book of Good Foods* mentions a dish similar to the Bohemian Dalken, namely the "Pehamian Arbeiss," approximately "Bohemian Dough." This was a dessert with honey, crushed almonds, and spices that was served warm or cold. This "Bohemian Dough" could be called the precursor of the Bohemian *Dalken*, also known as *Liwanzen*. It is also interesting to note that a clumsy cook ruining a dish is known as the "*Dalkerter*" who botched it (*Dalken* is Austrian slang for a clumsy person to this day.)

Basic Palatschinken Recipe

Yields 6-7 *Palatschinken*

Stir together flour with a little milk, egg, lemon zest, vanilla sugar, and salt, gradually stir in remaining milk and—preferably with a hand blender—work into a smooth dough. Stir in melted butter. Allow dough to rest for about 15 minutes.

Use the dough to fry thin *Palatschinken* in hot butter.
Note: Keep *Palatschinken* warm until filling.

Note: Batter may be diluted by the addition of milk, since it shrinks a little after resting.

just under 1 cup (90 g) flour (fine)
¾ cup (180 ml) milk
1 egg
peel of ½ lemon (untreated), zested
½ tsp vanilla
sugar pinch of salt
1 tbsp (15 g) melted butter
butter for frying

Cream Dalken

Currant Sauce: Remove stems from currants, wash, and drain well. Bring 3 tbsp of water to a boil with remaining ingredients, add currants, return to a boil, remove from heat, and let cool.

Prepare vanilla sauce according to the recipe on p. 259.

Cream Dalken: Separate eggs. Stir sour cream with yolks, lemon zest, flour, and salt until smooth. Beat egg whites with granulated sugar until stiff. Stir $1/3$ of the egg whites into the batter mix, fold in the rest. Heat fat in an egg or *Dalken* frying pan; using a tablespoon, place portions of dough into the indentations and fry on both sides for about 2 minutes over low heat.

Note: If the fat is too hot, the *Dalken* will brown too quickly and remain raw inside.

Put together two *Dalken* each with currant sauce, sprinkle with sugar, and serve with vanilla sauce.

Tip: Cream *Dalken* also taste wonderful with marinated strawberries, blueberries, or raspberries.

Yields 8 servings

Cream Dalken
4 eggs
½ cup ($1/8$ l) sour cream
peel of ½ lemon (untreated), zested
just under 1 ¼ cup (120 g) flour (fine)
pinch of salt
½ cup (100 g) of granulated sugar

Currant Sauce:
3 ½ heaping cups (400 g) currants
¾ cup (150 g) granulated sugar
2 cl (1–2 tbsp) cassis (currant liqueur)

Vanilla Sauce:
See recipe (p. 259)
½ cup (100 g) ghee or clarified butter*
powdered sugar for sprinkling

*Clarified butter: Slowly melt butter. Skim rising foam from the surface.

Kaiserschmarren

Yields 2 servings

Schmarrenteig:
2 tbsp raisins
4 eggs
just under 1 ¼ cup (120 g)
flour (fine)
pinch of salt
1 tsp vanilla sugar
⁷/₈ cup (200 ml) milk
peel of 1 lemon (untreated),
zested
2 ½ tbsp (30 g) granulated
sugar
¼ cup (60 g) clarified butter
for frying
powdered sugar for sprinkling

Wash raisins in hot water and drain well. Separate eggs. Mix flour with salt, vanilla sugar, milk, lemon zest, and yolk in a bowl and stir to a smooth dough. Puree dough with hand mixer (to avoid clumps).

Beat egg whites with granulated sugar until stiff. Stir ¹/₃ of the egg whites into the batter. Fold remaining egg whites into batter.

Heat butter in a frying pan, pour in *Schmarrenteig*, sprinkle with raisins, and fry until the underside is golden brown. Then quarter the dough and turn each quarter with a spatula or dough scraper. Bake *Schmarren* in preheated oven at 400°F (200°C) for about 10 minutes until done.

Remove pan from oven, shred *Schmarren* using two forks, sprinkle with powdered sugar, and serve. Serve *Palatschinken* with applesauce (recipe, p. 260) or plum sauce (recipe, p. 261).

Topfen Schmarren with Strawberry Sauce

Yields 2 servings

3 eggs
¹/₃ heaping cup (80 g) Topfen
(10% fat),
strained a little over ¹/₃ cup
(90 ml) whipping cream
¼ cup (60 ml) milk
peel of ½ lemon (untreated),
zested
pinch of salt
1 tsp vanilla sugar
¾ cup (80 g) flour (fine)
2 ½ tbsp (30 g) granulated
sugar
¼ cup (60 g) butter or clarified
butter
powdered sugar for sprinkling

Separate eggs. Stir together yolk with *Topfen*, whipping cream, milk, lemon zest, salt, vanilla sugar, and flour. Beat egg whites with granulated sugar until stiff, and stir ¹/₃ into the *Topfen* mixture. Fold in remaining egg whites.

Heat butter in a pan, pour in *Schmarren* dough, and fry for about 3 minutes until the underside is golden brown. Then turn dough with a spatula or dough scraper. Bake in preheated oven at 400°F (200°C) for about 15 minutes until done.

Remove pan from the oven, shred *Schmarren* using two forks, let cool for a moment, and sprinkle with powdered sugar.

Serve with strawberry sauce (recipe, p. 256).

Coconut Schmarren

Yields 4 servings

Schmarrenteig:
not quite 1 cup (70 g) shredded coconut
4 eggs
¾ cup (80 g) flour (fine)
1 tsp vanilla sugar pinch of
salt
½ cup (⅛ l) milk
2 ½ tbsp (30 g) granulated
sugar
¼ cup (60 g) butter or clarified
butter

Rum Sauce:
½ cup (⅛ l) milk
½ tsp vanilla pudding powder
1 egg yolk
2 ½ tbsp (30 g) granulated
sugar
1 tsp vanilla sugar
1 tbsp rum
2 tbsp raisins
powdered sugar for sprinkling

Rum Sauce: Mix vanilla pudding powder with some of the milk, stir in egg yolks. Bring remaining milk to a boil with granulated and vanilla sugars. Stir in vanilla-yolk milk, bring to a boil, and cook until it thickens while constantly stirring. Stir in rum. Wash raisins in hot water, drain well, dry on absorbent paper, and stir into the sauce just before serving.

Schmarrenteig: Distribute shredded coconut evenly on a baking sheet and lightly brown in the oven at 400°F (200°C); immediately shake onto a plate so that the coconut doesn't continue to darken and let cool. Separate eggs. Stir yolk with flour, vanilla sugar, salt, and milk until smooth; if lumps form, puree batter with a hand blender or strain through a sieve. Beat egg whites with granulated sugar until stiff and fold into the shredded coconut.

Heat clarified butter in a pan, pour in *Schmarrenteig*, and fry until the underside is golden brown. Then turn dough with a spatula or dough scraper. Bake in preheated oven at 400°F (200°C) for about 10 minutes until done.

Remove pan from oven, shred *Schmarren* using two forks, arrange each portion with rum sauce, sprinkle with sugar, and serve.

Bohemian Dalken

Dampfl: Crumble yeast and dissolve in ½ cup (¹/₈ l) warm milk, stir to a thick porridge with some flour, dust with a little flour dust, and let rise covered in a warm place (about 77–82°F or 25–28°C) to twice the volume.

Separate eggs. Stir together egg yolks, remaining milk, lemon zest, and salt and then mix well with the *Dampfl*. Beat together a smooth *Germteig* with the remaining flour and melted butter. Beat egg whites with granulated sugar until stiff and fold in. Cover dough and let rise in a warm place for about 15 minutes.

Heat fat in an egg or *Dalken* frying pan; using a tablespoon, place portions of dough into the indentations and fry on both sides over low heat. **Note:** If the fat is too hot, the *Dalken* will brown too quickly and remain raw inside.

Put together two *Dalken* each with *Powidl*, sprinkle with powdered sugar, and serve.

Yields 8 servings

1 ²/₃ tbsp (30 g) fresh yeast
½ cup (¹/₈ l) lukewarm milk
2 ½ cups (250 g) flour (fine)
2 eggs
peel of ½ lemon
(untreated), zested
pinch of salt
about 3 tbsp (40 g) melted butter
¼ cup (50 g) granulated sugar

Filling:
²/₃ cup (200 g) Powidl plum jam
(or cranberry sauce or jam)
½ cup (100 g) ghee or clarified butter*

*Clarified butter: Slowly melt butter. Skim rising foam from the surface.

Grießschmarren with Stewed Plums

Yields 2 servings

Schmarrenteig:
2 tbsp raisins
a little over 2 cups
(½ l) milk
pinch of salt
peel of ½ lemon (untreated),
zested
1 ²/₃ tbsp (20 g) granulated
sugar
2 tsp vanilla sugar
just under ¾ cup (120 g)
wheat semolina
2 egg yolks
2 tbsp butter or clarified butter

Stewed Plums:
See recipe (p. 261)

Schmarren: Wash raisins in hot water, drain well. Bring milk to a boil with salt, lemon zest, granulated and vanilla sugars, stir in semolina, and boil until thick and creamy; remove from heat and let cool briefly. Then stir in egg yolks and raisins.

Meanwhile, prepare plum sauce (recipe, p. 261).

Melt butter in a heatproof pan. Crumble semolina mixture and brown in the butter, and then bake until crispy brown in a preheated oven at 400°F (200°C) for about 20 minutes.

Note: During baking, keep turning the *Schmarren* over and shredding it. Serve with stewed plums.

Chocolate Nut Palatschinken

Yields 5 servings

Palatschinkenteig:
Basic recipe (p. 74)

Filling:
½ cup (¹/₈ l) milk
½ cup minus
1 tbsp (80 g) granulated sugar
2 ¹/₃ cups (200 g) walnuts,
ground
pinch of cinnamon (ground)
3 tbsp rum

Chocolate Sauce:
Recipe chocolate sauce 2 (p. 258)

Filling: Boil milk with sugar, stir in walnuts and cinnamon, briefly roast nut mixture, and add rum for flavor.

½ cup (¹/₈ l) whipping cream 1 tsp vanilla sugar 1 cup (80 g) walnuts, coarsely chopped, for sprinkling

Prepare chocolate sauce (recipe p. 258).

Palatschinken: Fry according to basic recipe (p. 74), spread with nut filling, fold into triangles, and keep warm.

Beat whipping cream with vanilla sugar until creamy and pour into a pastry bag with a serrated tip. Coat half of the *Palatschinken* with chocolate sauce, decorate with whipped cream, sprinkle with walnuts, and serve.

Germpalatschinken

Germpalatschinken: *Dampfl:* Slightly warm ¼ cup (¹/₁₆ l) milk and stir together with crumbled yeast, about 2 tablespoons of flour, and a pinch of sugar. Sprinkle with a little flour, cover, and let rise in a warm place about 15 minutes The volume should double. Separate eggs. Stir yolk with salt, melted butter, remaining flour, and *Dampfl* until smooth. Beat egg whites with granulated sugar until stiff and fold in. Use the dough to fry *Palatschinken* in hot fat. Keep *Palatschinken* warm for filling.

Filling: Stir together *Topfen* with sour cream, powdered sugar, lemon zest, vanilla mixture, and salt. Whip cream until stiff and fold in.

Raspberry Sauce: Prepare as described on p. 256.

Coat one *Palatschinken* each with *Topfen* filling and raspberry sauce, fold *Palatschinken*, sprinkle with powdered sugar, and serve. **Note:** *Palatschinken* can also be baked in the oven until they're done: Pour batter into the pan, start frying on the stove and then bake in a preheated oven at 350°F (180°C) until done. Using this method the *Palatschinken* rise especially nicely and get very fluffy.

Variation: Fill with *Powidl*, cranberry, or apricot jam.

Yield about 6 servings

Germpalatschinken:
½ tbsp (10 g) yeast a little over
¾ cup (³/₁₆ l) milk
1 cup (100 g) flour(fine)
pinch of sugar
3 eggs
pinch of salt
2 tbsp melted butter
peel of ½ lemon (untreated), zested
1 tsp vanilla sugar butter for frying

Topfen Filling:
²/₃ cup (150 g) *Topfen* (20 % fat),
strained 3 tbsp sour cream a little over
¹/₃ cup (50 g) powdered sugar
peel of ½ lemon (untreated), zested pinch of salt
¹/₃ cup (80 ml) whipping cream
pulp of 1 scraped out vanilla pod

Raspberry sauce:
See recipe (p. 256)

Coconut Palatschinken with Stewed Apricots

Yields 6 servings

Palatschinkenteig:
$^2/_3$ cup (50 g) shredded coconut
½ cup ($^1/_8$ l) milk
¾ cup (80 g) flour (fine)
3 tbsp melted butter
1 egg
1 egg yolk
pinch of salt
1 tsp vanilla sugar
butter for frying

Stewed Apricots:
Recipe (p. 260)

Distribute shredded coconut evenly on a baking sheet and lightly brown in the oven (this helps the aroma to unfold).

Puree shredded coconut with milk—preferably with a hand blender. Stir flour, butter, egg yolk, salt—and vanilla sugar into the coconut milk. **Note:** If lumps form, briefly puree with the hand blender. Allow *Palatschinken* dough to rest for about 15-20 minutes.

Stewed Apricots: Prepare according to the recipe (p. 260).

Use the dough to fry thin *Palatschinken* in hot butter. **Note:** Keep *Palatschinken* warm until filling. Fill *Palatschinken* with stewed apricots, fold in triangles, sprinkle with sugar—and serve.

Tip: These go very well with whipped cream and/or vanilla, apricot—or coconut ice cream.

Apricot *Palatschinken*

Yields 10 *Palatschinken*

Palatschinkenteig:
Basic recipe (p. 74)

approximately
$^1/_3$ heaping cup (120 g) apricot jam
powdered sugar for sprinkling

Fry *Palatschinken* according to the basic recipe (p. 74). Keep *Palatschinken* warm by stacking them and covering with foil.

Then coat *Palatschinken* with jam, roll together, sprinkle with powdered sugar, and serve.

Topfenpalatschinken

Fry the *Palatschinken* as in the recipe on p. 74 and set aside in a stack.

Filling: Wash raisins in hot water, drain well, and dry on absorbent paper. Separate eggs. Press *Topfen* through a sieve. Stir soft butter together with powdered and vanilla sugars, cornstarch, salt, and lemon zest until frothy. Gradually stir in yolk and *Topfen*. Beat egg whites with granulated sugar until stiff and fold into the *Topfen* mixture with the raisins.

Lay out *Palatschinken* in an overlapping row so that one contiguous surface results. Spread *Topfen* mixture evenly—possibly applying with a pastry bag (see illustration)—and roll up *Palatschinken* into a long roll. Cut roll into 10 pieces.

Stack *Palatschinken* in a buttered casserole dish and bake in a preheated oven at 325°F (160°C) for about 15 minutes.

Topping: Mix all ingredients until smooth, pour over *Palatschinken,* and bake an additional 25 minutes.

Prepare vanilla sauce according to the recipe (p. 259). Divide *Palatschinken* into portions, sprinkle with sugar, and serve with vanilla sauce.

Yields 5 servings

Palatschinkenteig:
Half the quantity of the recipe on p. 74

Topfen **Filling:**
1 ounce (30 g) raisins
3 eggs
$^7/_8$ cup (200 g) *Topfen*
¼ cup (50 g) soft butter
$^1/_3$ cup (50 g) powdered sugar
1 tsp vanilla sugar
2 tsp cornstarch
pinch of salt
peel of ½ lemon (untreated), zested
¼ cup (50 g) granulated sugar
butter for the mold

Topping:
½ cup ($^1/_8$ l) milk
½ cup ($^1/_8$ l) sour cream
2 eggs
¾ cup (30 g) powdered sugar
1 tsp vanilla sugar
pinch of salt

Vanilla Sauce:
Basic recipe (p. 259)
powdered sugar for sprinkling

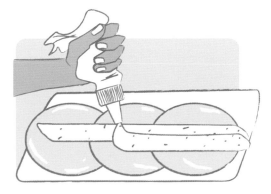

Orange Omeletten

Omelettenteig:
4 oranges (untreated)
4 eggs
1 ½ cups (150 g) flour (fine)
$^7/_8$ cup (200 ml) milk
peel of ½ orange (untreated), zested
1 tsp vanilla sugar
pinch of salt
2 ½ tbsp (30 g) granulated sugar
¼ cup (60 g) fat (butter is best) for frying

Orange Cream Sauce:
½ cup ($^1/_8$ l) whipping cream
¼ cup (50 ml) orange juice
juice of ½ lemon
½ cup minus 1 tbsp (80 g) granulated sugar
peel of ½ orange (untreated), zested
2 egg yolks
1 tbsp orange liqueur

powdered sugar for sprinkling

Omelettenteig: Finely zest the peel of 1 ½ oranges (**Note:** The zest of ½ orange is for the orange cream sauce). Peel all of the oranges with a sharp knife so that the white skin is also removed. Fillet oranges and dry orange slices on paper towels.

Separate eggs. Stir yolk with flour, milk, orange zest, vanilla sugar, and salt until smooth. Beat egg whites with about ½ tbsp granulated sugar until soft peaks form and fold in.

Heat clarified butter in small pans (about 4 inches [10 cm] in diameter). Pour dough in portions and fry briefly; remove from heat and place orange slices evenly on the dough, sprinkle with a little granulated sugar, and finish baking the omelets in a preheated oven at 400°F (200°C) for about 10 minutes.

Orange Cream Sauce: Beat whipping cream to a creamy consistency and chill. Stir orange juice with lemon juice, sugar, zest of ½ orange, and yolks until thick and creamy and beat warm; remove from heat and continue beating until it has reached room temperature (="beat cold").

Then fold in whipped cream and orange liqueur and refrigerate the sauce.

Pour orange cream sauce into soup bowls, place *omelettes* on top, sprinkle with sugar, and serve.

Palatschinken with Caramelized Apple Slices

Yields 5 servings

Filling:
a little over 1 lb (½ kg) apples
juice of ½ lemon
1 tbsp butter
½ cup (100 g) granulated sugar
2 tbsp apple liqueur or brandy

Cream Sauce:
½ cup (⅛ l) chilled whipping cream
1 tsp powdered sugar
2 cl (2–3 tbsp) apple liqueur

Palatschinkenteig:
Recipe (p. 74)

powdered sugar for sprinkling

Filling: Wash apples, quarter and remove seeds, and cut into $^2/_5$ inch (1 cm) thick slices. Drizzle apple slices with a few drops of lemon juice.

Melt butter. Lightly caramelize sugar in it, deglaze with remaining lemon juice and apple liqueur, and stir well. Add apple slices and cook in the caramel until soft.

Note: Instead of apple liqueur (or brandy), you can also use apple juice.

Cream Sauce: Beat chilled whipping cream with powdered sugar and apple liqueur until thick and chill.

Fry *Palatschinken* according to recipe (p. 74), fill with apple wedges, and fold in triangles. Place *Palatschinken* on warmed plates in portions, sprinkle with powdered sugar, and briefly bake in the oven on high broil or under the grill.

Note: This will lightly caramelize the powdered sugar and coat the *Palatschinken* with a delicate layer that crackles when cutting. Serve with cream sauce.

Tip: This also goes perfectly with vanilla ice cream.

Baked Apricot Palatschinken

Palatschinkenteig: Stir together flour with some of the milk, egg, yolk, vanilla sugar, lemon zest, salt, and melted butter; gradually stir in remaining milk so that a thin batter results. Puree *Palatschinken* dough with a hand blender or press through a sieve and let rest for 20 minutes.

Filling: Wash apricots, remove pits, cut into slices, and dry thoroughly on absorbent paper.

Bring ½ cup (¹/₈ l) water to a boil with granulated sugar, lemon juice, cinnamon stick, and vanilla sugar. Insert apricot slices and cook until soft (but don't let them fall apart). Remove cinnamon stick and strain the apricot slices, collecting the juice. Puree about a quarter of the apricots with a little juice. Mix the remaining apricots in with the puree.

Cream: Stir together vanilla pudding powder with 4 tbsp of coffee cream and the yolks. Bring remaining coffee cream with granulated and vanilla sugars, butter, and salt to a boil. Slowly stir in yolk-vanilla pudding mixture and let simmer, stirring constantly, until creamy; remove from heat and blend in the blender on low until the cream has cooled to room temperature. Cover and chill this base cream until needed.

Fry up *Palatschinken* from the *Palatschinken* dough in hot fat and stack to keep warm. Place on *Palatschinken* on each plate and spread on apricot filling. Fold *Palatschinken* in triangles. Stir base cream with apricot liqueur until smooth. Beat whipping cream until creamy and fold in. Pour cream over the *Palatschinken*. **Important:** Wipe plate edges well with a damp paper towel so nothing can catch on fire during browning.

Bake *Palatschinken* in a preheated oven at 500°F (250°C) (broil) until golden brown.

Yields 4–6 servings

Palatschinkenteig:
¾ cup (80 g) flour (fine)
about ½ cup (¹/₈ l) milk
1 egg
1 egg yolk
1 tsp vanilla sugar
peel of ¼ lemon (untreated), zested
2 tbsp melted butter or oil salt butter or clarified butter for frying

Filling:
4 ½ cups (700 g) apricots
½ cup (100 g) granulated sugar
juice of 1 ½ lemons
1 cinnamon stick
1 tsp vanilla sugar

Cream:
1 tsp vanilla pudding powder
1 cup (¼ l) coffee cream (15% fat)
2 egg yolks
3 ¹/₃ tbsp (40 g) granulated sugar
1 tsp vanilla sugar
2 ¾ tbsp (40 g) butter
pinch of salt
4 cl (3 tbsp) apricot liqueur
¼ cup (60 ml) whipping cream

Palatschinken Torte

Yields one Torte (8 pieces)

Poached Pears:
4 pears (preferably Bartlett)
$^2/_3$ cup (120 g) granulated sugar
juice of 1 lemon
4 cl (2–3 tbsp) Williams liqueur

Nut Filling:
$^7/_8$ cup (200 ml) milk
½ cup (100 g) granulated sugar
3 ½ cups (300 g) walnuts, ground
1 pinch cinnamon (ground)
4 cl (2–3 tbsp) rum

Palatschinkenteig:
Recipe (p. 74)

Williams Sauce:
1 ½ tbsp (12 g) vanilla pudding powder
1 cup (¼ l) milk
1 egg yolk
$^1/_3$ cup (70 g) granulated sugar
pinch of salt
2 cl (1–2 tbsp) Williams liqueur

Poached Pears: Wash pears, peel, halve, remove seeds. Bring granulated sugar with lemon juice, Williams liqueur, and ½ cup ($^1/_8$ l) water to boil. Put in pear halves and cook until al dente. Let pears cool in the broth; then remove, drain well, and cut into thin slices.

Nut Filling: Bring milk with sugar to a boil. Stir in nuts and cinnamon and briefly roast; remove from heat, stir in rum, and let the filling cool. **Note:** If the filling is too solid, dilute with a little milk.

Palatschinken: Fry as described in the recipe (p. 74) and let cool.

Williams Sauce: Stir vanilla pudding mix with a little cold milk and egg yolk until smooth. Bring remaining milk with sugar and salt to a boil. Pour vanilla-yolk milk into boiling milk while stirring; cook until creamy while stirring constantly. Allow to cool, stir in Williams liqueur. Puree the sauce with a hand blender.

Note: If the sauce is too thin, possibly add a little whipped cream and stir until it thickens.

Place a *Palatschinken* on a Torte platter, spread a thin layer of the nut mixture on it, place a few pear slices on it, cover with a *Palatschinken,* and repeat the process until all ingredients are used up. Finish with a *Palatschinken*, possibly decorate with pear slices, and serve with Williams sauce.

Apple Pasty

Yields about 8-10 servings

Palatschinkenteig:
Basic recipe (p. 74)

Filling:
a little over 3 lb (1 ½ kg) apples (such as Golden Delicious)
1 cup (¼ l) apple juice
½ cup minus
1 tbsp (80 g) granulated sugar
peel of ½ lemon (untreated), zested
juice of 1 lemon
½ cinnamon stick
3 sheets of gelatin

Caramel Sauce:
2 tsp vanilla pudding powder
1 cup (¼ l) milk
¾ cup (150 g) granulated sugar

Cinnamon Cream:
1 cup (¼ l) whipping cream
pinch of cinnamon (ground)
powdered sugar

Prepare 8 *Palatschinken* as described in the recipe (p. 74) and chill.

Filling: Wash apples, peel, core, and cut into a little over ½ inch (1.5 cm) thick slices. Bring apple juice to a boil with 1 cup (¼ l) water, sugar, lemon zest and juice, cinnamon stick, then add slices and cook until al dente. Strain and collect the juice. Drain apple slices on a wire rack and let cool. Soak gelatin in plenty of cold water. Bring ½ cup ($1/_8$ l) of the broth to a boil. Squeeze out gelatin well and dissolve in the warm juice. Mix in apple slices.

Cover a *Rehrücken* mold (literally "saddle of venison," which a well-known Austrian pastry resembles, see recipe p.) with clear plastic wrap. Fill out the mold with *Palatschinken* in such a way that the *Palatschinken* hang a bit over the edge of the mold.

Add apple filling to the mold and spread smoothly. Fold overhanging *Palatschinken* over the filling so that it is completely covered. Cover with foil and chill for at least 2 hours—preferably overnight.

Caramel Sauce: Stir vanilla pudding powder with some cold milk until smooth; heat remaining milk to about 175°F (80°C). Heat a pan, lightly brown about ¼ of the sugar, add another ¼ of the sugar (reduce heat if necessary), and caramelize until light brown; continue until all of the sugar is used up and lightly browned. Immediately douse with half of the milk mixture. **Careful:** The milk will boil up strongly, so the pan must be fairly large. Pour in remaining milk. Let stand until the caramel is completely dissolved (It may be necessary to puree with a hand blender until no more lumps are present.). Add vanilla pudding milk and cook while constantly stirring until a creamy sauce results.

Cinnamon Cream: Beat whipping cream with cinnamon and a little powdered sugar until it thickens slightly. Turn out pasty from the mold onto a cutting board, cut in slices with a sharp knife, and serve with caramel sauce and cinnamon cream. Garnish with chopped almonds.

Bilberry Cookies

Yields 6 servings

Cookie Dough:
1 ⅓ cup (200 g) bilberries
3 eggs
¾ cup (80 g) flour (fine)
pinch of salt
1 tsp vanilla sugar
about ¼ cup ($1/16$ l) milk
2 ½ tbsp (30 g) granulated
sugar
¼ cup (60 g) clarified butter

Bilberry Sauce:
Half the quantity of the recipe
on p. 256

Bilberry Sauce: Prepare half the quantity of the recipe as described on p. 256.

Cookie Dough: Select the best bilberries, wash, and drain well on absorbent paper. Separate eggs. Mix flour with salt, vanilla sugar, milk, and yolks until smooth. Beat 2 egg whites with granulated sugar until stiff and fold into the batter. Fold in well-drained bilberries.

Heat fat in a frying pan. Add dough in portions using a tablespoon and fry both sides over low heat.

Arrange bilberry sauce on plates, add bilberry cookies, and serve with vanilla ice cream.

*Known as *Heidelbeeren,* these are often confused with ordinary blueberries, which work fine as a substitute.

Nut Palatschinken with Red Wine Cherries

Yields 5 servings

Palatschinkenteig:
See recipe (p. 74)

Filling:
½ cup (¹/₈ l) milk
½ cup minus
1 tbsp (80 g) granulated sugar
2 ¹/₃ cups (200 g) walnuts,
ground
pinch of cinnamon (ground)
3 tbsp rum

Red Wine Cherries:
See recipe (p. 261)

Red Wine Cherries: Prepare according to the recipe on p. 261.

Filling: Boil milk with sugar, stir in walnuts and cinnamon, briefly roast nut mixture, and add rum for flavor.

Palatschinken: Fry according to the basic recipe (p. 74), spread with nut filling, fold into triangles, and keep warm.

Serve *Palatschinken* with red wine cherries.

Small Topfen Pancakes with Applesauce

Yields 6 servings

Topfen **Pancakes:**
1 cup (250 g) Topfen (10% fat)
peel of ½ lemon (untreated),
zested
pinch of salt
1 egg
1 egg yolk
1 tsp vanilla sugar
not quite 3 tbsp (30 g) wheat
semolina
¹/₃ cup (30 g) flour (fine)

Applesauce:
See recipe (p. 256)
a little over 2 cups (½ l) fat
for frying
3 tbsp granulated sugar cinnamon (ground)
sour cream for garnish

Topfen Pancakes: Press *Topfen* through a sieve with a dough scraper. Melt the butter and let cool a bit. Stir together *Topfen* with butter, lemon zest, salt, egg, yolk, and vanilla sugar. Gradually stir in semolina and flour. Let *Topfen* mixture rest for about 1–2 ½ hours.

In the meantime, prepare applesauce according to the recipe on p. 256.

Cut out small portions from the *Topfen* dough with a tablespoon and form *Knödel* with moistened hands, flatten slightly and fry the pancakes in hot fat over medium heat (about 300°F ([150°C]) until golden.

Remove *Topfen* pancakes with a straining ladle and drain well. Mix granulated sugar with cinnamon and sprinkle the *Topfen* pancakes. Serve *Topfen* pancakes with applesauce and a dab of sour cream.

Fried Pastries

The pastry kitchen, as opposed to the confectionery, is likely an invention of women who usually remained anonymous. Although a certain legendary Cecilia Krapf supposedly existed to whom the invention of the *Krapfen* (donut) is ascribed, as a matter of fact, even the ancient Romans were already familiar with donut-like baked goods: Mention can be found of a mushy dough that was cooked in hot fat and then coated with honey. It was a baked good infused with a love spell, baked for the riotous spring *bacchanalia* and consumed in huge quantities. Roman colonists probably brought the dish to the Danube *Limes* (ancient Roman border) and to Vindobona. It took a Viennese pastry cook to take this acquired specialty and make it into a cult favorite.

Today's **Krapfen** most likely got their name from their original hooked shape. Even at the time of Karl the Great, the term *krapho* meant something hooked, a curved claw. No one knows exactly what was meant by the native term; even today, different pastry forms are known as "*Krapfen*," whether round, spherical, oblong, curved or plaited, sweet or savory, unfilled or filled with meat, cabbage, spinach, fish, fruit, nuts, or jam, whether served warm or cold. But one thing they all have in common, namely that they are cooked in hot fat, mainly in melted butter. *Butterkrapfen* (butter), Zottelkrapfen (strip), *Bauernkrapfen* (farmer), *Brandteigkrapfen* (choux pastry), *Ischler Krapfen* (from the town of Bad Ischl), *Schlickkrapfen* (mud), *Spießkrapfen* (skewer), *Prügelkrapfen* (beaten), *Schmerkrapfen* (lard), *Husarenkrapferln* (hussar), *Rosenkrapfen* (rose) . . . this random selection shows how widely and arbitrarily the word *Krapfen* was applied in subsequent cookbooks. The jam-filled *Krapfen* are likely a product

of the bourgeois culinary arts. We can no longer determine when these *Krapfen* became round and received a bright ring in the middle, but this spherical shape can already be found in the "Fried Mice."

Fried pastries—no matter what kind—always played a major part in everyday rustic food, but even more so on feast days. Their size, shape, and filling were determined by the occasion. Making "Fried Mice" required less fat and eggs, so they were originally mainly festive food for poorer people. In a food regulation for servants from 1749, the following instructions were written: "Extra for the carnival meal to each person three *Krapfen*!" It is striking that pastries fried in fat were always served on happy feast days, but rarely on sad occasions. *Krapfen*, *Strauben* (funnel cake), and *Küchlein* (a type of donut) still make for an exuberant, happy mood—it is the irresistible aroma that comes from the frying of the sweet goodies.

Fried pastries can be made from *Germteig* (yeast dough), *Brandteig* (choux pastry dough), *Weinteig* (wine dough), *Bierteig* (beer dough) as well as from *Mürbteig* (shortcrust pastry dough). They can be filled or unfilled, but must always be consumed as fresh as possible.

When frying the correct frying temperature is crucial for success. Between 275 and 310°F (140 and 160°C) is ideal, depending on the size of the frying equipment. The thicker the dough pieces, the lower the frying temperature, so the outside does not brown too quickly before they are cooked through on the inside. Let the fried goods drain thoroughly on several layers of paper towels. This didn't used to be necessary as the fat content was very important for heavy physical labor.

How to make your Krapfen succeed:

♦   All ingredients should be at room temperature. Even the flour! Take the eggs, butter, and milk out of the refrigerator with plenty of time to spare—at least 1 hour before.
♦   I also recommend straining the flour, which makes it more airy and easier to mix with the other ingredients, making the dough rise better.
♦   The so-called *Dampfl* (Austrian term for the pre-ferment), i.e., the fermentation test for the yeast is not absolutely necessary, but one can immediately determine if the yeasts are "doing their job."
♦   Yeast dough should be well beaten and strongly kneaded and needs time to rest and rise. The oven is the ideal place for the dough to rise. Preheat to 125°F (50°C) and then shut off.
♦   The dough will have especially fine pores if it is beaten after rising and then left to rise again. Repeat the sequence.
♦   When forming the *Krapfen*, there are two different schools of thought, as with many traditional dishes, whose followers each believe themselves to be in possession of the "only true method:" For so-called "rolling," the dough is divided into individual portions and then rolled into smooth, round balls using the palms. The "rolled" *Krapfen* is easier to handle for beginners. It is filled only after baking.
    Scooped out *Krapfen* are made of two dough slices stuck together with jam.
♦   It is best to use unflavored vegetable or coconut oil, even if these are not necessarily the least expensive. Particularly fine are *Krapfen* that have been fried in clarified butter. The expenditure is worth it!
♦   The frying temperature is ideal at 300–310°F (150–160°C). Check the temperature! **Tip:** Moisten a wooden spoon handle and place it in the hot fat; if bubbles form, then the fat is hot enough and the *Krapfen* can be immersed. *Krapfen* should always be placed with the risen side down into the fat. Do not put in too many *Krapfen*! Cover the pot so that the steam created helps the *Krapfen* to rise nicely. After about 1 ½ minutes, lift the lid, and if the underside is nice and golden, flip the *Krapfen* and finish frying with the lid off. Remove from the fat with a slotted spoon and drain well on absorbent paper.

- Perfectly fried *Krapfen* bear a seal of approval around their round middles: a uniform white ring, also called the "*Ranftl.*" The secret? The rum. It not only provides flavor, but the alcohol that evaporates during frying also helps the *Krapfen* to rise nicely. The air in the *Krapfen* gives it some "lift" and lets it easily swim on the surface.
- To fill the *Krapfen,* there are special *Krapfen* tips for commercial pastry bags.
- Now that nothing can go wrong, one last tip from me: Sprinkle the still-warm *Krapfen* with sugar and enjoy.

The words *Pavese, Pofesen, Poföse, Bofese* in Middle High German described a large shield topped with a long iron point that was driven into the earth to provide protection for archers. Even today, the Italian name for two shield-shaped white bread slices put together with a filling is "*Pavese.*" The first occurrence of the word can be traced to the *Tegernsee* monastery cookbook from the year 1534.

The dish consists of two bread slices that are filled—depending on the recipe—with calf brain or *Powidl* (plum jam) and fried in an egg coating. Brain *Pofesen* are probably the reason why the human brain in the Viennese dialect is also called "*Pofesen* chamber."

The following should be observed when frying *Pofesen*:

♦ For frying on the surface of the oil, you need a relatively high frying temperature: between 310 and 350°F (160 and 180°C) is ideal, depending on the size of the frying equipment. This causes a crispy crust to form immediately after placing into the hot fat. At too low of a temperature, the *Pofesen* immediately soak up as much fat as they will hold, making them soft instead of crunchy.

♦ Only fats that can be heated to a high temperature such as clarified butter, lard, coconut oil, or oil should be used.

♦ **Note:** Don't heat the fat so much that it begins to smoke. Smoking fat is too hot and should not be used because it is harmful to health.

♦ Let the fried *Pofesen* drain thoroughly on several layers of paper towels. This didn't used to be necessary as the fat content was very important for heavy physical labor.

Fried Apple Slices with Cider Cream

Yields 6 servings

1 $^2/_3$ lb (¾ kg) apples
juice of 1 lemon
2 tbsp rum or brandy
2 tbsp powdered sugar

Weinbackteig:
See recipe (p. 108)
a little over 2 cups (½ l) fat
for frying

Cider Cream:
½ cup ($^1/_8$ l) apple cider
3 $^1/_3$ tbsp (40 g) granulated
sugar
4 egg yolks
pinch of salt
1 tsp vanilla sugar
a little over ½ cup (150 g)
cranberry sauce
powdered sugar for sprinkling

Wash apples, peel, core, and cut apples into about $^2/_5$ inch (1 cm) thick slices. Sprinkle apple slices with lemon juice, rum, and powdered sugar, and let stand for a while.

Prepare *Weinbackteig* according to the recipe on p. 108.

Dip apple slices in the batter and fry both sides in hot fat for about 3 minutes until golden yellow. Remove with a straining ladle and drain well.

Cider Cream: Stir together apple cider with sugar, yolks, salt, and vanilla sugar in a mixing bowl, and beat over steam with a whisk until frothy.

Arrange fried apple slices with cider cream and 1 tbsp each of cranberry sauce, serve sprinkled with powdered sugar.

Schlosserbuben

Bring red wine to a boil with ½ cup ($1/8$ l) of water, sugar, cinnamon stick, and lemon and orange zest, and let stand over low heat for about 5 minutes.

Remove pits from prunes if necessary (but don't cut them in half), place in the broth, and let stand over low heat about 5 minutes; remove from heat. Remove orange and lemon zest from the broth and chill the plums for at least 6 hours—preferably overnight.

Drain the prunes well and stuff with an almond (or piece of marzipan).

Prepare *Backteig* according to the recipe on p. 263.

Drag plums through the batter and fry in hot fat. Drain well on absorbent paper.

Prepare raspberry sauce according to the recipe on p. 256.

Mix chocolate with powdered sugar and roll the *Schlosserbuben* in it, serve with raspberry sauce while still hot.

Note: For children, only marinate the *Schlosserbuben* in water!

Variation: You can also marinate the prunes in a mixture of rum and slivovitz.

Schlosserbuben is another descriptive term, meaning "locksmith boys"!

Yields 4 servings

¼ cup ($1/16$ l) red wine
$1/3$ cup (60 g) granulated sugar
½ cinnamon stick
peel of each of ½ a lemon (untreated)
and ½ an orange (untreated), zested
36 prunes
18 peeled almonds or about 1 cup (200 g) marzipan (cut in small pieces)

Backteig:
Recipe (p. 263)

Raspberry Sauce:
See recipe (p. 256)
a little over 2 cups (½ l) fat for frying
$7/8$ cup (90 g) dark chocolate couverture, grated
$2/3$ cup (90 g) powdered sugar

Fried Mice

about 1 ²/₃ cups (160 g) flour
(fine)
¹/₃ cup (80 ml) milk
just under ½ tbsp (8 g) yeast
2 egg yolks
1 tbsp powdered sugar
1 tsp vanilla sugar
pinch of salt
peel of ½ lemon (untreated),
zested
2 heaping tbsp (30 g) butter
a little over 2 cups (½ l) oil or
shortening for frying
powdered sugar for sprinkling

Sift flour. Heat milk until lukewarm (about 75°F [25°C]). Crumble yeast and stir to a porridge with the milk and some of the flour; dust with flour, cover, and let rise to one and a half times its volume in a warm place.

Stir together yolks with powdered and vanilla sugars, salt, lemon zest, and then work into a smooth, soft dough—preferably with a hand mixer dough hook—together with the *Dampfl*, remaining flour, and at the end, the butter. Cover and let rise to one and a half times its volume in a warm place.

Heat fat in a pot (medium heat, about 300°F [150°C]). Using a tablespoon repeatedly dipped in the hot fat, scoop out small portions, submerge in the hot fat, and fry each portion until crispy and golden yellow over low heat about 2 minutes. Remove with a straining ladle and drain well on absorbent paper. Serve with powdered sugar.

Tip: Serve with fruit sauce (e.g., raspberry or strawberry sauce).

Vienna Faschingskrapfen

Yields about 12 *Krapfen*

2 ¾ tbsp (50 g) fresh yeast
about 1 cup plus
1 tbsp (140 ml) milk
6 ½ cups (650 g) flour (fine)
5 egg yolks
2 eggs
¼ cup (50 g) granulated sugar
2 ½ tbsp (20 g) vanilla sugar
just under ¼ cup (55 ml) rum
¾ heaping tbsp (12 g) salt
peel of ½ lemon (untreated),
zested
½ cup plus
1 tbsp (130 g) soft butter
flour for preparing
just under ½ cup (150 g)
apricot jam
just under 3 cups (600 g)
shortening
(preferably coconut shortening)
powdered sugar

Dissolve yeast in lukewarm milk and stir to a porridge with a little flour; dust with some flour; cover *Dampfl* and let rise in a warm place (max. 77–82°F or 25–28°C) until it has doubled in bulk and the surface begins to crack.

Stir together yolks with eggs, granulated and vanilla sugars, rum, salt, and lemon zest. Gradually stir in the soft butter together with the *Dampfl* and the remaining flour and work into a smooth dough—preferably with a hand mixer dough hook. Cover dough and let rise in a warm place for about 10 minutes.

Roll out dough on a floured work surface about $2/5$ inch (1 cm) thick. Sweep off excess flour. Cut out 12 slices (each 2 $1/3$ inches [6 cm] diameter) from one-half of the dough. Mark 12 circles on the rest of the dough with a cookie cutter. Add 1 tsp apricot jam to each. Place the cut out slices on top and press down slightly. Using a cookie cutter, smoothly cutout the *Krapfen* and place them facedown on a floured cloth; cover and let rise in a warm place.

Note: They should expand by about $1/3$.

Place *Krapfen* in hot fat (300°F [150°C]*) with the curved side down, cover, and fry for about 3 minutes. Turn *Krapfen* with a wooden spoon, cover, and finish frying for about 3 more minutes until both sides have the same color. Remove *Krapfen* with a draining ladle and drain well on a wire rack or several layers of paper towels. Let cool. Sprinkle with powdered sugar and serve.

*To test the proper temperature, stick a moistened fork into the oil—if it starts to moderately spatter and hiss, then it is the right temperature

Wäschermädel

Yields 6 servings

18 fully ripe apricots
1 tbsp powdered sugar
about 1 cup (200 g) marzipan
4 cl (2–3 tbsp) apricot liqueur
½ cup (50 g) sliced almonds

Apricot Sauce:
about 2 cups (300 g) apricots
3 ⅓ tbsp (40 g) granulated
sugar
juice of ½ lemon
½ cinnamon stick

Weinbackteig:
2 eggs
1 ⅓ cup plus
1 tbsp (140 g) flour (fine)
½ cup (⅛ l) white wine
peel of ½ lemon (untreated),
zested
2 tbsp oil
pinch of salt
2 ½ tsp (10 g) granulated
sugar
a little over 2 cups (½ l) oil or
neutral-tasting shortening
powdered sugar

Wash apricots, blanch, rinse in ice water, and peel. Core apricots using a wooden spoon handle (place wooden spoon handle at the stem and force out pit). Sprinkle apricots with powdered sugar in a bowl, mix well, and let stand for about ¼ hour.

Prepare apricot sauce in the meantime: Wash apricots, remove pits, and cut into quarters. Bring ¼ cup (¹/₁₆ l) water to a boil with apricots and remaining ingredients and cook over medium heat until the apricots are very soft. Remove cinnamon stick, puree sauce, and if desired flavor to taste with lemon juice and sugar.

Weinbackteig: Separate eggs. Puree flour, white wine, lemon zest, oil, and salt, preferably with a hand blender. Beat 2 egg whites with granulated sugar until soft peaks form and fold into the batter. Remove apricots from the marinade and drain well on a wire rack; then pat dry.

Mix marzipan with apricot liqueur, cut into 18 pieces, and stuff the apricots with the marzipan pieces in place of the pits.

Dip apricots in the batter, sprinkle sliced almonds over the apricots, and fry swimming in hot fat over medium heat for about 2 minutes. Drain well on absorbent paper. Sprinkle with powdered sugar and serve with apricot sauce.

Wäschermädel, another descriptive term, meaning "washer maids."

Pofesen (Arme Ritter) with Warm Berries

Yields 4 servings

8 slices of loaf bread suitable
for toasting*
3 tbsp (60 g) Powidl plum jam

Vanilla Milk:
½ cup (⅛ l) milk
1 tsp vanilla sugar
pinch of salt
peel of ½ orange (untreated),
zested
2 eggs
1 ⅛ cup (250 g) oil for frying
3 tbsp granulated sugar
cinnamon (ground)
powdered sugar

*You can also use bread rolls or
brioche.

With a cookie cutter, cut out circles from the slices of bread of about 3 inches (8 cm) in diameter. Spread *Powidl* on 4 circles of bread on one side each. Place one uncoated disc of bread onto each coated disc of bread and carefully press together with your hands.

Whisk milk with vanilla sugar, orange zest, salt, and egg. Briefly (several seconds!) submerge the two pieces of bread in the vanilla milk and fry until crispy swimming in hot oil.

Drain *Powidl-Pofesen* on a wire rack well. Mix granulated sugar with cinnamon and sprinkle the *Pofesen*. Cut *Pofesen* in half diagonally, arrange on plates, sprinkle with powdered sugar and serve, preferably with warm berries.

Arme Ritter is the conventional German term for what we call French toast, literally translating as "poor knight," as in that was all they could afford to eat!

„Pofesen, Pofesen,wo bist du gewesen?
Im Himmel sechs Wochen, die Teuferln tun kochen,
die Engerln tun lachen, dass die Buckerln tun krachen!"
Translation:
"Pofesen, Pofesen, where have you been?
In heaven six weeks, where the devils do cook,
The angels are laughing and the humpbacks are cracking!"
Were the devils in this song boiling with rage since they weren't able to eat with everyone else, or were they starting up their own hellish competition?

Cold
Mehlspeisen

Coffee Mehlspeisen

"Kaffeejausen," the Austrian term for a light meal or snack, have become rare. This is a shame, for they are an attractive form of hospitality, gathering many generations around a table.

Jause sounds old-fashioned, but the term has a touchingly humorous sound to it and also reflects a bit of longing for peace and relaxation. It is much more than a snack and a more active break than a siesta.

The *Jause* is a feudal invention that became prevalent at the Viennese court in the thirteenth century at the time of King Premysl Otakar, when fortune still smiled upon him and the Habsburgers had not yet plotted his demise. Originally, the *Jause* was a snack around lunchtime, only later was it moved to the afternoon. It was a pretty sumptuous meal that could only be afforded by the court and the bourgeoisie. The word comes from the Old Czech "*Jouzina,*" which was later adopted into Viennese. *Jause* also contains the word "*Jug*" for south, familiar from the Yugoslavian.

People used to "*jaus*" before the Turkish invasion, to which we owe coffee, and before the Spanish explorers, cocoa—only back then it was wine and smoked meats instead of coffee and pastries. *Brettljausen* (little board snacks), where you enjoy bacon and ham, are still just as popular today in rural areas, where they are a reward for hard work after a mountain tour. *Teejausen* (tea snacks) have not really prevailed, although tea is gaining in popularity.

So many an Austrian fate was decided over coffee and *Gugelhupf*: the *Jause* with "*gnädige Frau Schratt*" was an institution. At the *Jause* table with her friend, the journalist Berta Zuckerkandl, Schratt was informed of the terrible fate of her friend and colleague Alexander Girardi. Poor Girardi was being threatened with committal to an asylum. After an argument with his scheming wife, he had had a breakdown and threatened suicide. Even as police and ambulances were surrounding his house, he fled in a false beard and a white wig to Schratt. She pulled all the stops to liberate Girardi from his wife's web of intrigue, even the Kaiser was informed. And the consequences did not only benefit Girardi, but fundamentally reformed legislation. Ever since then, not only doctors but also a judge must agree to a psychiatric committal.

. . . *Gugelhupf, Strudel, Golatschen, Beugel, Potizen, Cremeschnitten, Indianerkrapfen, Torten,* and *Buchteln* are the fluffy and light foundation of a fare that only became associated with regret once we started to count calories.

It was the many Bohemian cooks who ensured the earthiness of the Viennese pastry kitchen by "importing" yeast dough. *Buchteln* came to us at a time when Bohemia was still part of Austria. "*Buchticky*" or "*Buchta*" was their name there. They became popular—as Franz Maier-Bruck explored—in *Biedermeier* Vienna. A resourceful and enterprising innkeeper at the *Agnes Bründl* on *Hermannskogel* hill was deliberating on how he could increase sales of his *Buchteln*. Instead of filling them with boiled fruits or *Powidl* (plum jam), he filled the yeast dough treat with numbered tickets from the lottery (known at the time as "*Terno*") and sold them for a reasonable price. The Viennese, who make an annual pilgrimage to *Hermannskogel* on January 21, St. Agnes day, and August 29, the day John was beheaded, were delighted. All of Vienna bought *Ternobuchteln*!

Filled with jam or *Powidl, Buchteln* are the quintessential Viennese coffee pastries. *Dukatenbuchteln* (ducat dumplings) have an especially refined reputation. They are made of fluffy yeast dough, scooped out the size of a ducat—an antiquated Austrian currency—and fried without filling.

Yeast dough is culturally and historically one of the oldest ways to bake cakes. What once occurred by chance (the forgotten dough that began to ferment) was refined over the course of time. The principle is the same: Under favorable temperatures and in a moist nutrient solution, live yeasts convert the starch of the flour into sugar, which then breaks down into alcohol and carbonic acid. Carbon dioxide seeks to escape the confines of the dough and drills small holes through which it emerges—thus the dough expands, it "rises." Although yeast dough has a firm place in the Austrian pastry kitchen, the use of yeast is not that old. Not until the seventeenth century was liquid beer yeast used for making white bread and breadrolls. Compressed yeast was first produced in Vienna in 1867. In Austria, they used the word *Germ* for yeast (instead of the German word "*Hefe*"), which is derived from "*gären*" (ferment).

Germteig (yeast dough) is the most versatile of all types of dough, and depending on the ingredients, it can become a solid house pastry or a refined delicacy.

◆ The use of fresh yeast is important for success, which only is able to have its effect at pleasantly warm temperatures.

◆ Cold drafts are detrimental to the delicate yeast dough, so we cover it up to keep it from "catching cold." Heat is good for yeast dough, ideally 75–95°F (25–35°C), but too much heat has the opposite effect—above 110°F (43°C), the yeast cells die and the dough won't rise! The live yeasts dislike direct contact with fat or salt, which inhibits growth. Yeast dough is most successful when all of the ingredients are mixed warm.

◆ When using dry yeast, the specified amount of yeast should be increased by about 25% (1 package of dry yeast is equivalent to about 1 ounce of fresh yeast). Fresh yeast can be frozen up to 4 months without loss of quality.

◆ Yeast dough preparation without a pre-ferment ("*Dampfl*") is called the straight dough method, whereas preparation of a *Dampfl* is known as the indirect dough method (or sponge method). Mix the yeast in a container with a little sugar, add some warm milk and some flour, and stir it until smooth. Sprinkle with flour, cover, and let the pre-ferment rise for about 15 minutes at about 75°F (25°C) until it has doubled in bulk and the surface begins to crack. Knead this *Dampfl* together with the entire amount of flour and the other (also lukewarm!) ingredients and knock the dough vigorously until it is smooth and shiny. The long and exhausting working through process has been greatly simplified by food processors. Subsequently cover and let the dough rise at approximately 82–90°F (28–32°C) until it has doubled in bulk.

◆ **Tip:** An electric oven is an ideally warm place for rising, best when preheated at the lowest level at max 100°F (40°C), or a gas oven preheated at the lowest level for a few minutes and then turned off and allowed to cool slightly.

◆ Use fine flour (sifted), and if it was stored cold, it should be stored at room temperature for about ½ a day before using or briefly warmed in the oven (up to 100°F [40°C]).

◆ For *Buchteln*, shape the dough into a roll and cut it in slices or cut out pieces (2 1/3 inches [6 cm] diameter) with a cookie cutter from the dough flattened to a thickness of about a ¾ inch (2 cm).

◆ Fill each dough piece with a teaspoon of jam or *Powidl* filling.

◆ Fold dough disks in the middle, turn in melted butter, and place them with the closed side down into the mold.

Basic Blätterteig Recipe

Yields about 5 ½ lbs (2 ½ kg) dough

Pre-Ferment:
about 2 ¼ lb (1 kg) flour (fine)
2 cups (480 ml) water
1 ½ tbsp (22 ml) rum
1 ⅛ tbsp (17 g)
salt ½ cup (100 g) oil

Butter Brick:
3 ½ cups (800 g) butter
just under 1 ¼ cup (120 g) flour (fine)
flour for preparing

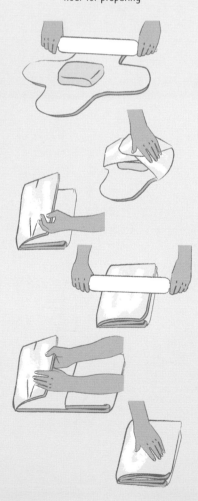

Pre-Ferment: Sift flour onto a work surface; make an indentation in the center. Add water, rum, salt, and butter into the well and knead with the flour into a smooth, firm, shiny dough. Form dough into a ball, cut an X into the ball, wrap in a damp paper towel, and let rest for about ¾ hour (do not refrigerate!).

Butter Brick: Using a knife, chop well-chilled butter into smaller pieces, knead with flour, and shape into a "brick" (10 inches [25 cm] length) on a lightly floured surface with a dough scraper, then chill for about 45 minutes. Carefully roll out the pre-ferment on a floured surface using a rolling pin, the corners a little thinner, the center a little thicker. Sweep away excess flour. Place the butter brick in the middle of the four-layer dough, and one after the other, fold over the four dough layers over the butter brick.

Then roll out dough to a rectangle.

Simple Method: Fold over one-third of the dough from both left and right to the center so that now three layers of dough are lying atop one another.

Double Method: Turn dough 90 degrees and then roll out into a rectangle again. Fold over one quarter of the dough from both left and right to the center and then fold over in the center again so that now four layers of dough are lying atop one another. Cover dough and let rest at least 45 minutes in a cool place and repeat the simple and double methods. Cover dough again, and let rest for about 1 hour in the refrigerator.

Then follow the appropriate recipe.

Important: Always roll out *Blätterteig* ⅓–¾ inches (1–2 cm) further than needed, since *Blätterteig* contracts a bit during baking!

Blätterteig was allegedly already known to the ancient Egyptians, but was almost certainly already being made in the Middle Ages in northern Italy.

Blätterteig (literally "leaf dough," comparable to phylo dough or puff pastry dough) is a simple pastry dough that is layered with fat (if butter is used, it is known as Butterteig), folded and rolled out again. This process of folding in on itself (one distinguishes between the simple and double methods) can be repeated as many times as desired—the more often you do it, the finer the dough. Due to the fat, air bubbles form between the dough layers during baking, resulting in the individual layers easily separating from each other and the dough becoming very light and crispy. These layers are the special characteristic of the dough, known as "mille feuille" in France—a thousand leaves. Blätterteig does not contain sugar and can therefore be used for both sweet and savory pastries.

Here are some tips to help make Blätterteig successful at home too:

◆ It is best to go ahead and prepare a lot of the Blätterteig because working accurately is important, which is easier with larger quantities.

◆ The ingredients should be processed cold when possible (use butter straight from the fridge).

◆ It can be helpful to let Blätterteig cool before working with it.

◆ Only work on the dough on lightly floured, cool work surface, so the ratio of the ingredients is not changed.

◆ Always precisely observe rest breaks between the "rounds" so that the dough can relax. If the breaks are too short, it will contract.

◆ Only use sharp knives and cutters for cutting, otherwise the dough edges will be compressed and the rising of the dough will be prevented.

◆ Blätterteig gets a nice surface through brushing with whisked egg yolks (for longer baking times use egg whites so that the surface doesn't become too dark). However, one shouldn't brush the dough edges, since they will cause the dough layers to stick together and prevent complete or even rising.

◆ Do not knead Blätterteig remnants back together, but layer them atop one another, press lightly together, chill briefly, and then roll out again with a rolling pin. This way the dough layering remains intact and the dough can rise.

◆ Blätterteig can be kept for two days in the refrigerator or frozen.

◆ Blätterteig is baked on a baking sheet sprinkled with water at high baking temperatures (depending on the size of the pastry at about 400–425°F [200–220°C]).

◆ Pastries will rise particularly well if a vessel of water is placed into the oven as well—the resulting steam gives the pastry additional lift.

◆ **Important:** Always serve Blätterteig fresh!

Basic Recipe Plunderteig

Yields about 2 ¾ lbs (1 ¼ kg) dough

Butter Brick:
1 ½ cups (350 g) butter
½ cup (50 g) flour (fine)

Pre-Ferment:
5 cups (½ kg) flour (fine) just under 2 tbsp (35 g) yeast
about ⅞ cup (200 ml) milk
3 ⅓ tbsp (40 g) granulated sugar
1 tsp vanilla sugar
pinch of salt
egg yolk
peel of 1 lemon (untreated), zested
2 heaping tbsp (30 g) butter
flour for preparing

Butter Brick: Using a knife, chop well-chilled butter into small pieces, knead well with flour, and shape into a "brick" 4 inches x 8 inches (10 cm x 20 cm) on a lightly floured surface using a dough scraper; cover and chill.

Pre-Ferment: Sift flour into a bowl. Crumble yeast and stir together with ½ cup (⅛ l) cold milk, sugar, and vanilla sugar until the yeast has dissolved completely. Knead yeast with flour, salt, yolks, remaining milk and lemon zest, and butter into a smooth, pliable dough. Place dough on a floured plate, cut an X into it and let rest about 5 minutes. Roll out dough from the center on a floured work surface with a rolling pin. Place the butter brick in the middle of the four-layer dough and one after the other fold over the four dough layers over the butter brick and firmly press the dough ends together. Then roll out the dough into a rectangle, starting from the center. Fold over one-third of the dough from both left and right to the center so that now three layers of dough are lying atop one another. Wrap dough in plastic wrap and refrigerate about 20 minutes.

Place dough with the long side down on the work surface and roll out and layer again as described above. Then let dough rest for about 30 minutes in the refrigerator.

Basic Recipe Brandteig (Krapfen, Profiteroles, Eclairs)

Yields about 10 pieces

just under ½ cup (100 ml) water
just under ¼ cup (55 g) butter
pinch of salt
⅔ cup (70 g) flour (fine)
2 eggs

Bring water to a boil with chopped butter and salt. Stir in flour and cook, stirring constantly, until the dough detaches from the bottom of the pot. Remove from heat. Pour flour into a bowl. Stir in eggs, preferably with a hand blender.

Then proceed with the individual recipe.

Brandteig: "Put lard and water into a pan, boil, pour into some nice flour and beat three eggs into it . . . " This old recipe for "*Aufgeloffene Hasen-Oehrlein*" ("fried rabbit ears") from the *New and Useful Cook-Book* shows that *Brandteig* is not an invention of the modern pastry kitchen, but rather that people have prepared sweets and traditional cakes from it for centuries.

Its name comes from the fact that for the preparation of the dough the flour was not used raw, but rather "*abgebrannt*" or "burned off" (*Brand* literally means blaze).

Tips:

- Milk or water? If the dough is baked in an oven, then the *Brandteig* is prepared with water; if it is to be fried in oil—for example, for *Krapfen*—use milk.
- Cook the dough until the dough begins to detach from the bottom of the pan and a white layer has formed on the bottom of the cookware.
- If the dough is baked in the oven or fried in oil, whole eggs are used in the burned-off dough. For boiling, e.g., in fruit *Knödel* or *Powidl* pockets, use only the yolk.
- Especially important for the preparation of *Brandteig* is the precise quantification of the amount of egg to be mixed in with the "burned off" dough. Even one egg too many can spoil the dough—it will no longer hold together and becomes lumpy. Therefore, the best thing to do is to whisk the eggs you think you will require and gradually mix them into the somewhat cooled dough (hand mixer). This way you can more easily dose the adding of the eggs. Sometimes it may be necessary to deviate from the amount of eggs specified in the recipe once the dough has reached the right consistency.
- The dough has the right consistency if it is smooth and firm.
- Oven: Close the door!!! Don't open the oven door during baking—the dough is still not fixed and will collapse.
- Eat immediately! Since *Brandteig* pastries can only be stored for a maximum of one day, it is best to leave them uncovered on the baking sheet. Never put in foil or tin cans or Tupperware—they will turn tough in a very short time.
- *Brandteig-Krapfen* should not be filled until immediately before serving, because the filling softens the dough quickly.
- The unfilled fried donuts can be easily frozen. Thaw at room temperature for about 30 minutes, then briefly warm in an oven preheated to about 375°F (190°C).

Strawberry Cream Schnitten

Yields 6 servings

Blätterteig:
about ½–⅔ lb (250-300 g) of the basic recipe (p. 118)
½ lb (250 g) strawberries for the filling

Cream Mixture:
3 gelatin sheets
4 egg whites
a little less than 1 cup (180 g) granulated sugar
powdered sugar for sprinkling

Blätterteig: Prepare according to the recipe on p. 118. Roll out *Blätterteig* into a $1/_{12}$ inch (2 mm) thin rectangle 12 x 8 inches (12 ½ inches [32 cm] x 8 inches [20 cm]). **Note:** Always roll out *Blätterteig* ¾ inch [2 cm] further than needed, since it contracts a bit during baking. Place onto a baking sheet lined with parchment paper and prick with a fork several times (= *stupfen*). Bake in preheated oven at 400°F (200°C) for about 25 minutes. The *Blätterteig* should be well baked, it may be necessary to let it finish at about 250–275°F (130–140°C). Let cool.

Carefully cut *Blätterteig* lengthwise into 2 parts 12 x 3 inches (12 inches [30 cm] x 8 cm). Place one strip onto a baking sheet lined with parchment paper and secure with an adjustable pastry frame.

Wash and trim strawberries, dry very well, and line up according to length in the center.

Cream Mixture: Soak gelatin in cold water. Beat egg whites warm over steam (approximately 104°F [40°C]) with granulated sugar, remove from heat and then beat cold (until the mixture has reached room temperature and the egg whites are very stiff). Dissolve gelatin over steam and very quickly and briefly (!) stir into the egg whites.

Immediately fill egg white mixture into a pastry bag with a smooth tip and pipe onto the *Blätterteig* base prepared with strawberries in the pastry frame. Smooth the surface. Let stand for about 30 minutes (to thicken). Then carefully detach the pastry frame from the mixture on the edge using a knife dipped in hot water and remove. Turn the second *Blätterteig* strip so that the "nice" side is up, cut into six strips (2 inch [5 cm] wide) and place on the cream slices. Using a moist serving knife, cut portion slices and sprinkle decoratively with sugar.

Buchteln

Germteig:
1.5 ounces (40 g) yeast
4 ounces (120 ml) lukewarm milk
5 cups (500 g) flour (fine)
3 egg yolks
1 egg
¼ cup (50 g) granulated sugar
1 tsp vanilla sugar about
½ tbsp (8 g) salt
3 tbsp (45 ml) rum
peel of ½ lemon (untreated), zested
½ cup (100 g) soft butter flour for preparing
approximately 1 cup (300 g) Powidl plum jam
butter for the mold and melted butter for brushing
powdered sugar

Germteig: Crumble yeast and dissolve in the lukewarm milk, stir to a porridge with some flour, dust with flour, and let rise covered in a warm place for about 15 minutes.

Note: The volume should double and the surface should show coarse cracks.

Stir yolks with egg, granulated and vanilla sugars, salt, rum, and lemon zest until frothy. Add the soft butter, *Dampfl,* and the remaining flour and work into a smooth, soft dough—preferably with a hand mixer dough hook. Cover dough and let rise to double its volume in a warm place for about 20 minutes.

Knead yeast dough through again on a floured surface, roll out $^1/_5$ inch (½ cm) thick and cut into squares 2 $^1/_3$ x 2 $^1/_3$ inches (6 cm x 6 cm). Using a pastry bag with a smooth tip, add a dab of *Powidl* to each piece, or use a spoon to put a small dab of *Powidl* on each piece. Twist dough closed over the filling and place with the seam down into a buttered mold. Brush with melted butter and let rise at about 82–86°F (28–30°C) to almost double the volume, then bake in a preheated oven at 350°F (180°C) for about 35 minutes. After baking, brush with butter again and let cool about 5 minutes.

Sprinkle *Buchteln* with sugar and serve with vanilla sauce (recipe, p. 259).

Kärntner Reindling

Yields one *Reindling* with 10
pieces

***Germteig* (this quantity is
enough for 2 *Reindlinge*):**
1 ounce (30 g) yeast
4 ounces (120 ml) lukewarm
milk
5 ½ cups (550 g) flour (fine)
3 egg yolks
1 egg
¼ cup (50 g) granulated sugar
1 tsp vanilla sugar
about ½ tbsp (8 g) salt
3 tbsp (45 ml) rum
peel of ½ lemon
(untreated), zested
½ cup (100 g) soft butter flour
for preparing

Filling:
1 cup (150 g) raisins
½ tsp cinnamon (ground)
½ cup (100 g) whole cane
sugar*
²/₃ cup (50 g) walnuts,
coarsely chopped
butter for the mold and for
brushing
flour for preparing

*With whole cane sugar, the
Reindling tastes more refined; of
course you can also use ordinary
granulated sugar.

Germteig: Crumble yeast and dissolve in the lukewarm milk, stir to a porridge with some flour, dust with flour, and let rise covered in a warm place for about 15 minutes.

Note: The volume should double and the surface should show coarse cracks. Stir yolks with egg, granulated and vanilla sugars, salt, rum, and lemon zest until frothy. Add the soft butter, *Dampfl,* and the remaining flour and work into a smooth dough—preferably with a hand mixer dough hook. Cover dough and let rise to double its volume in a warm place for about 20 minutes.

Filling: Wash raisins in hot water and drain well. Mix cinnamon and sugar. Melt a little butter. Coat one *Gugelhupf* mold (preferably not ceramic) with butter.

Roll out yeast dough on a floured work surface into a rectangle about ¹/₅ inch (5 mm) thick, brush with butter, and sprinkle with cinnamon sugar, raisins, and walnuts. Roll up dough firmly, press the ends of the roll together so that a bit of a ring results, place in the mold, press lightly, brush with butter, cover with plastic wrap, and let rise for about 45 minutes. Bake in preheated oven at 325–350°F (170–180°C) for about 45–50 minutes.

Turn *Reindling* out of the mold and brush with melted butter again.

Nut Potize

Yields 2 *Potizen* with about 10 servings each

Germteig:
1 ounce (30 g) yeast
4 ounces (120 ml) lukewarm milk
5 ½ cups (550 g) flour (fine)
3 egg yolks
1 egg
¼ cup (50 g) granulated sugar
1 tsp vanilla sugar
about ½ tbsp (8 g) salt
3 tbsp (45 ml) rum
peel of ¼ lemon (untreated), zested
½ cup (100 g) soft butter
flour for preparing
melted butter for brushing

Nut Filling
⁷/₈ cup (210 ml) milk
²/₃ cup (120 g) granulated sugar
just under 2 tbsp (15 g) vanilla sugar
1 pinch of cinnamon (ground)
peel of ½ lemon (untreated), zested
3 ½ cups (300 g) walnuts, ground
a little less than 1 ¼ cup (70 g) breadcrumbs

Germteig: Crumble yeast and dissolve in the lukewarm milk, stir to a porridge with some flour, dust with flour, and let rise covered in a warm place for about 15 minutes.

Note: The volume should double and the surface should show coarse cracks. Stir yolks with egg, granulated and vanilla sugars, salt, rum, and lemon zest until frothy. Add the soft butter, *Dampfl,* and the remaining flour and work into a smooth dough—preferably with a hand mixer dough hook. Cover dough and let rise to double its volume in a warm place for about 20 minutes.

Filling: Bring milk to a boil with the sugar, vanilla sugar, cinnamon, and lemon zest. Stir in nuts and bread crumbs and roast for about 20 seconds. Immediately remove nut filling from the pot and let cool.

Knead yeast dough through again on a floured surface and shape into two equally large loaves. Roll out in a ¹/₅ inch (5 mm) thick rectangle. Distribute nut filling evenly on it and smooth out. Roll up dough from both sides to the center and place in a buttered and floured *Rehrücken* mold (about 12 inches [30 cm] long, 3 inches [8 cm] wide, 2 ¹/₃ inches [6 cm] deep); brush with melted butter and let rise for about 40 minutes in a warm place (86°F [30°C]). **Note:** The *Potize* should rise slowly, otherwise cavities form between the filling and dough. Bake in preheated oven at 350°F (180°C) for about 45 minutes. Let *Potize* cool and turn out from the mold.

Tip: *Potize* can also be made with poppy seed filling (p. 130).

Fine Mohnzopf

Yields one plait with 12 slices

Brioche Dough:*
2 eggs
just under ⅓ cup (40 g)
powdered sugar
just over ¾ tbsp (15 g) fresh
yeast
1 tsp vanilla sugar
just over 2 ¾ cups (280 g)
flour (fine)
½ heaping cup (125 g) soft
butter
⅓ tbsp (5 g) salt

Poppy Seed Filling:
1 ¼ cup (300 ml) milk
⅞ cup (110 g) sugar (pow-
dered)
½ package vanilla sugar
2 tbsp cinnamon
not quite ⅓ cup (50 g) wheat
semolina
1 ½ cup (200 g) ground poppy
seeds
butter for the loaf pan
hot apricot jam for spreading
fondant for glazing

*Brioche dough has a higher
butter content than normal yeast
dough.

Poppy Seed Filling: First prepare the filling so it can cool. Bring milk, sugar, vanilla sugar, and cinnamon to a boil, stir in wheat semolina, and let swell while constantly stirring. Add the poppy seeds, briefly roast, and let cool. **Note:** The filling should be spreadable. If it's too solid, add a little rum, sugar solution, or apricot jam.

Brioche dough: Stir together eggs with powdered sugar, crumbled yeast, and vanilla sugar until the yeast is completely dissolved and all ingredients are well mixed. Add flour and briefly knead; add salt, butter, and knead well into a smooth dough. Shape dough into a rectangle, cover with foil, and chill for about 15 minutes.

Roll out brioche dough into a rectangle (16 inches [40 cm] x 8 inches [20 cm]), spread filling on the lower half of the dough apply filling, fold over remaining dough, make diagonal cuts at regular intervals on two sides, and braid these strips into a *Zopf* (plait) (see illustration).

Place the *Zopf* in a buttered loaf pan and let rise by a third in a warm place (about 82°F [28°C]). Bake for about 55–60 minutes in a preheated oven at 325°F (165°C). Remove *Mohnzopf* from the oven, spread with hot apricot jam, and thinly glaze with fondant.

Tip: The *Mohnzopf* looks great if you sprinkle it with some more poppy seeds after baking.

 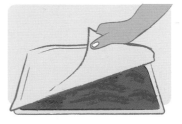

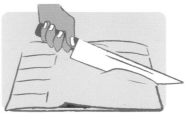 

Topfengolatschen

Yields 20

Plunderteig:
Basic recipe (p. 120)

Topfen Filling:
¼ cup (60 g) butter
2 ¼ cups (½ kg) Topfen, strained
peel of ½ lemon (untreated), zested
almost 1 cup (120 g) powdered sugar
1 egg
2 tsp cornstarch
1 tsp vanilla sugar
pinch of salt
flour for preparing
1 egg for coating
powdered sugar for sprinkling

Prepare *Plunderteig* according to the recipe on p. 120.

Filling: Melt butter. Stir *Topfen* with lemon zest, powdered sugar, butter, egg, cornstarch, vanilla sugar, and salt until smooth.

Roll out dough on floured work surface about $1/_{10}$ inch (2 ½ mm) thick. Cut out squares from the dough which are 4 inches (10 cm) to a side. Whisk egg and brush the dough edges with it. Place *Topfen* filling in small portions in the center of the dough. Pull the corners of the squares toward the center, fold over the filling, and press firmly. Cut small squares from the dough remnants and put them on the *Golatschen* as lids.

Place *Golatschen* far apart from each other on a baking sheet, cover with plastic wrap, and let rise for about 30 minutes in a warm place (about 86°F [30°C]). Bake in preheated oven at 350°F (180°C) for 15 minutes. Let the *Topfengolatschen* cool, remove from the baking sheet, and serve sprinkled with powdered sugar.

Fruchtplunder

Yields 20

Plunderteig:
Basic recipe (p. 120)

Vanilla Cream:
1 ²/₃ cups (200 g) of the recipe (p. 264)
various fruits
(also jarred fruits), berries, etc.
1 egg
1 package Torte jelly

Prepare *Plunderteig* (p. 120) and vanilla cream (p. 264) as described in the recipes.

Roll out dough on a floured surface about $1/_{10}$ inch (2 ½ mm) thick. Cut out 4 inch (10 cm) squares from the dough. Whisk egg and brush edges with it. Fill vanilla cream into a pastry bag with a smooth tip and pipe small portions onto the center of the dough. Pull two corners of the squares over the filling and press firmly. Place Plunder far apart from each other on a baking sheet, cover with plastic wrap, and let rise for about 30 minutes in a warm place. Then bake in preheated oven at 350°F (180°C) for 15 minutes. Prepare Torte jelly according to package instructions. Remove Plunder from the oven, layer with fruit, and brush fruit with jelly (= glaze).

Blätterteig Tarts with Apricots

Yields 6 servings

2 tbsp (40 g) sugar solution*
¾ heaping cup (150 g) raw
marzipan
4 cl (2–3 tbsp) apricot liqueur
about 3 ⁷/₈ cups (600 g)
apricots
½ lb (250 g) store-bought
Blätterteig
(or homemade *Blätterteig*
recipe, p. 118)
just under ¹/₃ cup (100 g)
apricot jam
²/₅ cup (50 g) pistachios

Vanilla Sauce:
1 cup (¼ l) milk
²/₃ cup (120 g) granulated
sugar
6 egg yolks
salt
1–2 tsp vanilla sugar

*Sugar solution: Bring water and
sugar to a boil in the ratio 1:1
and chill. Sugar solution can be
stored in a closed container in the
refrigerator for a few weeks.

First prepare vanilla sauce according to the recipe on p. 259. Blend sugar solution with raw marzipan and apricot liqueur to a smooth mixture. Wash apricots, drain well, remove pits, and cut into slices. Roll out *Blätterteig* about ½ inch (1 ½ mm) thick. Cut out pieces from the dough (4 ¾ inch [12 cm] diameter). Pull up *Blätterteig* edges slightly and fold inward about ¹/₅ inch (5 mm) wide so that a ridge results (small Torte edge). See illustration.

Spread *Blätterteig* sheets with the marzipan mixture. Place apricot slices on them with the cut side up and place the *Blätterteig* tarts on a baking sheet sprinkled with water; bake in a preheated oven on bottom rack at 450°C (230°C) for about 10 minutes. Bring apricot jam to a boil. Remove *Blätterteig* tarts from the oven, spread with hot jam, sprinkle with pistachios, and serve with vanilla sauce.

Note: It may be necessary to move the *Blätterteig* tarts up one rack during baking so that the bases don't get too dark. In order to check, briefly lift *Blätterteig* bases with a spatula.

Tip: Instead of apricots, plums are also perfectly suitable. If using these, stir together the marzipan mixture with slivovitz.

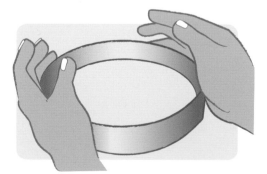

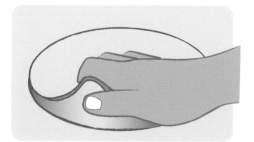

Schaumrollen

Yields 10-12

a little over 1 lb (500 g) store-
bought *Blätterteig*
(or homemade *Blätterteig*, p.
118)
flour for preparing melted
butter for brushing the molds

Cream Mixture:
3 egg whites
a little less than 1 cup (180 g)
granulated sugar
powdered sugar for sprinkling

Roll out dough on floured work surface in a rectangle about $1/10$ inch (2 ½ mm) thick. Remove flour from the surface with a dry brush. Cut *Blätterteig* into about 1 $1/8$ inch (1 $1/8$ inch [3 cm]) wide strips and brush these with water. Wrap one dough strip at a time overlapping around the *Schaumrollen* mold brushed with butter. Place the dough rolls with the seam side down onto a baking sheet lined with parchment paper (leave enough space between the *Schaumrollen* so they don't stick together), brush with whisked egg; let rest 10 minutes and then bake in a preheated oven at 410°F (210°C) for about 10 minutes. Reduce temperature to 400°F (200°C) and bake the rolls an additional 10-12 minutes.

Important: Don't open the oven door! Otherwise the dough won't rise as nicely!

Then turn off the oven, open the door a crack (wedge a wooden spoon in the door), and let the rolls continue to rise for about 10-15 minutes. Remove *Schaumrollen* from the oven, let cool (let rest a little longer if necessary), and gently detach from the molds.

Cream Mixture: Stir egg whites with granulated sugar over steam (about 104°F [40°C]) until frothy. **Important:** The sugar must have dissolved completely. Then—preferably with an electric mixer—beat cold. Fill cream mixture into a pastry bag with a smooth tip ($2/5$–½ inch [10-12 mm]) and fill the dough rolls via their small opening. Serve lightly sugared.

Important: *Butterteig* or *Blätterteig* must always be completely baked. If the *Schaumrollen* are still too soft or doughy on the inside, let them rest a little at about 250-275°F (130-140°C). Leave oven open a crack so that the moisture can escape.

Brandteigkrapfen

Yields 10 servings

Brandteig:
Basic recipe (p. 120)

Vanilla Cream:
See recipe (p. 241)

1 egg for coating
powdered sugar for sprinkling

Brandteig: Prepare according to the recipe on p. 120. Fill dough into a pastry bag with a large, serrated tip (no. 8) and pipe 10 rosettes (*Krapfen*) onto a baking sheet lined with parchment paper.

Important: Leave enough space between the *Krapfen*.

Brush *Brandteigkrapfen* with whisked egg and bake in a preheated oven at 210°C (375°F) for about 25 minutes. It might be necessary to turn the sheet and continue baking for several minutes. **Important:** Don't open the oven door during the first 25 minutes! Let *Brandteigkrapfen* cool completely on a wire rack. Cut cooled *Brandteigkrapfen* down the middle, fill with vanilla cream. Put *Krapfen* back together and sprinkle with powdered sugar.

Tip: *Brandteigkrapfen* also taste delicious with fresh fruits (e.g., strawberries).

Apple Crumble Cake

Mürbteig:
See recipe (p. 165)
flour for preparing
just under $^1/_3$ cup (100 g)
apricot jam

Biskuit Base (baking sheet sized 12 inches [30 cm] x 16 inches [40 cm]):
5 eggs
½ cup (100 g) granulated sugar
¼ package vanilla sugar
pinch of salt
peel of ¼ lemon (untreated), zested
½ cup (80 g) cornstarch
¾ cup (80 g) flour (fine)
$^1/_3$ cup (70 g) hot butter

Apple Filling:
1 $^1/_3$ cup (250 g) granulated sugar
4 g cinnamon
$^2/_3$ cup (100 g) starch (cornstarch)
just shy of 2 ¾ tbsp (40 ml) lemon juice
4 ½ lbs (2 kg) apple wedges, peeled
2/3 cup (100 g) raisins

Butter Crumbles:
2 ½ cups (250 g) flour (fine)
a heaping ¾ cup (180 g) butter, cut into small cubes
$^1/_3$ cup (60 g) raw marzipan, cut into small cubes
heaping $^2/_3$ cup (100 g) powdered sugar
pinch of baking powder
$^1/_3$ package of vanilla sugar
pinch of salt
pinch of cinnamon
a little over $^1/_3$ cup (50 g) powdered sugar
mixed with $^2/_3$ tbsp (5 g) vanilla sugar for sprinkling

Mürbteig: Prepare as described in the recipe on p. 165 and roll out $^1/_{10}$ of an inch (3 mm) thick to baking sheet size on a floured work surface or between sheets of parchment paper. Place on a baking sheet lined with parchment paper, prick with a fork several times (= *stupfen*, so that the pastry doesn't swell and rise irregularly). Bake in preheated oven at 350°F (180°C) for about 10 minutes until golden brown.

Biskuit Base: Stir together eggs with granulated and vanilla sugars, salt and lemon zest and beat over steam (104°F [40°C]) until thick and fluffy. Then beat cold. Sift both types of flour and fold in. Blend in hot butter.

Immediately brush mixture on a baking sheet lined with parchment paper; bake in a preheated oven at 400°F (200°C) for about 8–10 minutes. Let cool completely. Brush *Mürbteig* base with apricot jam. Put on *Biskuit* base with the "skin side" down, remove any baked-on paper, place a pastry frame around the *Biskuit*.

Apple Filling: Bring 2 ½ cups (600 ml) of water to a boil with granulated sugar and cinnamon. Stir cornstarch together with just under $^1/_3$ cup (70 ml) of water and lemon juice, add, and cook well, stirring constantly. Mix in apple wedges and raisins and cook until soft over low heat. **Note:** Repeatedly stir with a wooden spoon so the apple mixture doesn't burn. Then spread onto the *Biskuit* and smooth out. Let cool.

Butter Crumbles: Quickly knead all of the ingredients together and work into crumbles between your fingers. Chill for about 10 minutes, then place crumbles on a baking sheet lined with parchment paper and bake in a preheated oven at 325°–350°F (165–170°C) for about 18–20 minutes until golden brown. While still hot, chop to desired size with a spatula (dough scraper). Distribute evenly over the apple cake and sprinkle with vanilla-powdered sugar.

Plum Cake

Yields one baking sheet (16 inches [40 cm] x 12 inches ([30 cm]) with high edges

---

2 ²/₃ lbs (1.2 kg) plums
7 eggs
⁷/₈ cup (160 g) raw marzipan
just shy of 2 ¾ tbsp (40 ml) milk
just under ¾ cup (160 g) butter
just over ½ cup (70 g) powdered sugar
just under 2 tbsp (15 g) vanilla sugar
pinch of salt
peel of ½ lemon (untreated), zested
a little less than 1 cup (180 g) granulated sugar
¹/₃ cup (50 g) cornstarch
2 cups (200 g) flour (fine)
²/₃ cup (100 g) cornstarch
baking wafers
1 package clear Torte jelly

Wash plums and let dry. Then cut in half, remove pits, and make a small cut in each twice lengthwise.

Separate eggs. Stir raw marzipan with the yolks and milk in a pot—preferably with an electric mixer—until smooth and pour into a bowl. In the same pot, stir together butter, powdered and vanilla sugars, salt, and lemon zest until fluffy. Stir yolk mixture together with the butter mixture. Beat egg whites with granulated sugar and cornstarch until stiff, fold in to the butter-yolk mixture. Finally, mix in flour and cornstarch. Spread ¾ of the mixture onto a baking sheet lined with parchment paper. Cover with baking wafers and spread remaining mixture on top.

Top with the plums in the manner of overlapping roof tiles. Bake plum cake in preheated oven at 325°F (170°C) for about 45 minutes. Let cool.

Prepare Torte jelly according to package directions and brush plums with it (= so-called "glazing": the plums will stay fresh longer and the fruit won't darken further).

Note: The wafers keep the fruit from dropping down to the base.

Tip: This cake can also be topped with apricots, cherries, grapes, etc., in place of plums.

Cranberry Gugelhupf

Yields one *Gugelhupf* (2 liter mold)

2 cups (250 g) dried lingonberries or cranberries
just under ¼ cup (50 ml) egg liqueur
1 ⅓ cup (300 g) butter at room temperature
just over ½ cup (70 g) powdered sugar
2 tsp vanilla sugar
peel of ½ lemon (untreated), zested
a pinch of salt
6 eggs
1 ¼ cups (240 g) granulated sugar
3 cups (300 g) flour (fine)

Butter and sliced almonds for the *Gugelhupf* mold powdered sugar for sprinkling

Marinate cranberries with the egg liqueur for about 1–2 days.

Stir butter with powdered and vanilla sugars, lemon zest, and salt until frothy. Separate eggs. Gradually add yolks to the butter mixture. Beat egg whites with granulated sugar until stiff. **Note:** Beat well! Stir $1/_3$ of the egg whites into the butter mixture. Fold in remaining egg whites. Carefully fold in cranberries and flour. Pour into a buttered *Gugelhupf* mold sprinkled with sliced almonds, spread the batter to the top, and bake in a preheated oven at 325°F (170°C) for about 1 hour. Turn out the *Gugelhupf* from the mold, let cool, and serve sprinkled with powdered sugar.

Tip: To prevent the *Gugelhupf* from swelling over the edges of the *Gugelhupf* mold, place a strip of paper around the mold so that it pokes up above the edge by a few centimeters. Place a paper bag in the chimney (= hole in the mold).

Marble Gugelhupf

Separate eggs. Stir soft butter with powdered and vanilla sugars, lemon zest, and salt until creamy. Gradually add egg yolks.

Beat egg whites with granulated sugar until stiff. Stir $1/3$ of the egg whites into the butter mixture. Carefully fold in flour and the remaining egg whites. Stir together cocoa and oil. Pour $1/3$ of the *Gugelhupf* batter into another bowl and stir in the cocoa-oil to darken.

Alternate pouring the light and dark batters into a buttered *Gugelhupf* mold sprinkled with hazelnuts. Spread batter to the top (see illustration, p. 180) and bake the *Gugelhupf* in a preheated oven at 325°F (170°C) for about 1 hour. Turn out the *Gugelhupf* from the mold, let cool, and serve sprinkled with powdered sugar.

Yields one *Gugelhupf* with 10 slices

5 eggs
1 heaping cup (250 g) soft butter at room temperature
just under $2/3$ cup (80 g) powdered sugar
1 tsp vanilla sugar
peel of ½ lemon (untreated), zested
salt
¾ cup of granulated sugar
2 ½ cups of flour (fine)
1 tbsp cocoa
2 tsp oil
butter and sliced hazelnuts or flour for the pan
powdered sugar for sprinkling

Kaisergugelhupf

Yields one *Gugelhupf* (2 liter mold)

1 ⅓ cup (300 g) butter at room temperature
just over ½ cup (70 g) powdered sugar
2 tsp vanilla sugar
peel of ½ lemon (untreated), zested
a pinch of salt
6 eggs
1 ¼ cup (240 g) granulated sugar
1 ½ cups (140 g) chocolate, chopped into small pieces
1 ¼ cups (140 g) walnuts, chopped
3 cups (300 g) flour (fine)

butter and sliced almonds for the *Gugelhupf* mold powdered sugar for sprinkling

Stir butter with powdered and vanilla sugars, lemon zest, and salt until frothy. Separate eggs. Gradually add yolks to the butter mixture. Beat egg whites with granulated sugar until stiff.

Stir ⅓ of the egg whites into the butter mixture. Fold in remaining egg whites. Mix chocolate pieces with walnuts and flour and carefully mix in. Pour into a buttered *Gugelhupf* mold sprinkled with sliced almonds, spread the batter to the top, and bake in a preheated oven at 325°F (170°C) for about 1 hour.

Turn out the *Gugelhupf* from the mold, let cool, and serve sprinkled with powdered sugar.

Germgugelhupf

Yields one *Gugelhupf* cake
with 10 slices

Germteig:

just over 1 tbsp (20 g) yeast
½ cup (¹/₈ l) lukewarm milk
3 cups (300 g) flour (fine)
100 g raisins
4 egg yolks
½ cup minus
1 tbsp (80 g) granulated sugar
2 tsp vanilla sugar
peel of ½ lemon (untreated),
zested
pinch salt
¹/₃ cup (80 g) soft butter
butter and flour for the *Gugelhupf* mold
whole white almonds
powdered sugar for sprinkling

Germteig: Crumble yeast and dissolve in ¼ cup (¹/₁₆ l) lukewarm milk, stir to a porridge with some flour. Sprinkle *Dampfl* with flour, cover, and let rise in a warm place (about 82°F [28°C]) until it has doubled in bulk and the surface begins to crack. Wash raisins in hot water, dry on absorbent paper. Stir together yolks with remaining milk, granulated and vanilla sugars, lemon zest, and salt, stir in *Dampfl*. Add remaining flour and softened butter and beat everything into a smooth but firm yeast dough. Mix in raisins at the end.

Brush *Gugelhupf* mold with butter and sprinkle with flour. Place the white almonds on the bottom of the mold. Pour in dough, cover, and let rise in a warm place for about 45 minutes. Then bake in preheated oven at 325°F (170°C) for 45 minutes.

Turn out *Gugelhupf* from the mold and let cool. Serve sprinkled with sugar.

Nut Ring Cake

Mix flour with baking powder and sift. Separate eggs. Stir soft butter with powdered and vanilla sugars, salt, and rum until creamy. Gradually stir in egg yolks. Beat egg whites with a little granulated sugar until soft peaks form, drizzle in the rest of the sugar, and keep beating the egg whites until the sugar is completely dissolved. **Note:** Don't let the egg whites get too stiff.

Stir ½ of the egg whites into the butter mixture. Carefully mix in flour mixture, walnuts, and remaining egg whites.

Pour into a buttered ring cake mold sprinkled with bread crumbs, spread batter up to the edges (see illustration, p. 180), and bake cake in a preheated oven at 325°F (170°C) for about 1 hour. Turn out the cake from the mold, let cool, and serve sprinkled with powdered sugar.

Yields one cake with 12 slices

1 ¾ cups of flour (fine)
pinch of baking powder
1 heaping cup (250 g) soft butter at room temperature
6 eggs
$2/_3$ cup powdered sugar
1 tsp vanilla sugar
salt
1 tbsp rum
¾ cup (150 g) granulated sugar
2 $1/_8$ cups (180 g) walnuts, ground
butter and bread crumbs for the mold
powdered sugar for sprinkling

Whole Grain Cake

Yields 12 pieces (loaf pan 10 inches [25 cm] length)

Filling:
$^1/_3$ cup (40 g) pumpkin seeds
1 heaping cup (200 g) organic prunes

Whole Grain Batter:
1 ½ cups (190 g) whole wheat flour, ground
½ tbsp (5 g) baking powder
$^2/_5$ cup (75 g) raw marzipan
5 eggs
2 ½ tbsp (20 g) candied orange peel, chopped finely
¾ cup plus
1 tbsp (190 g) soft butter
scraped marrow from
1 vanilla pod
peel of ½ lemon (untreated), zested
salt
1 pinch of cinnamon (ground)
about 2 tbsp (40 g) whole cane sugar
2 heaping tbsp (45 g) honey
butter for the pan

Coarsely chop the prunes. Soak pumpkin seeds and prunes separately in warm water for at least 3 hours. Then pour off water, pat fruits and seeds dry with paper towels or dry the seeds in the oven at 175°F (80°C). **Note:** Reserve ¼ of pumpkin seeds for sprinkling in the mold.

Mix whole wheat flour with baking powder. Separate eggs. Stir marzipan with egg yolks and candied orange peel in a bowl until smooth.

Stir soft butter with vanilla extract, lemon zest, salt, and cinnamon until frothy. Stir into marzipan mixture. Beat egg whites with brown sugar and honey until stiff, fold in. Mix flour, prunes, and pumpkin seeds and carefully add.

Pour into a buttered loaf pan sprinkled with pumpkin seeds. Smooth the surface and place the whole wheat cake on the middle rack in a preheated oven at 375°F (190°C). Reduce temperature to 325°F (170°C) (convection: 310°F [160°C]) and bake the cake for about 35–40 minutes.

Banana Cake

Yields one cake with 14 slices

3 cups (300 g) flour (fine)
1 pinch of baking powder
3 eggs
1 ²/₃ cups (300 g) bananas*
1 ¼ cup (250 g) brown sugar
or
granulated sugar
2 tsp vanilla sugar
1 cup (¼ l) whipping cream
¹/₁₆ l oil
1 cup (80 g) of walnuts,
ground
butter and flour (or bread
crumbs) for the pan

*Note: Make sure to use overripe
fruit for this recipe so the cake will
be flavorful enough.

Mix flour with baking powder and sift. Separate eggs. Peel bananas and press through a sieve. Stir banana puree with sugar and vanilla sugar until fluffy. Gradually stir in yolks and cream. Finally, rapidly stir in the oil. Beat egg whites with granulated sugar until stiff. Stir ¹/₃ of the egg whites into the banana mixture; carefully fold in remaining egg whites, flour, and walnuts.

Pour into a buttered and floured mold, spread batter up to the edges (see illustration, p. 180), and bake cake in a preheated oven at 325°F (170°C) for about 45 minutes. Turn out cake from the mold and let cool.

Raisin Cake

Yields one cake with 12 slices

1 ¾ ounces of raisins
7 eggs
¾ heaping cup (160 g) granulated sugar
2 tsp vanilla sugar salt
peel of 1 lemon (untreated),
zested
2 ¾ tbsp (40 g) butter
butter and flour for the pan

Wash raisins in hot water and pat dry. Separate eggs. Stir yolks with 2 tbsp of granulated sugar, vanilla sugar, salt, and lemon zest until fluffy. Melt butter. Beat egg whites with remaining granulated sugar until stiff. Stir together ¹/₃ of the egg whites with the yolk mixture. Carefully fold in remaining egg whites and flour. Carefully mix in raisins and hot butter.

Pour into a buttered and floured loaf pan, spread batter up to the edges (see illustration, p. 180), and bake cake in a preheated oven at 325°F (170°C) for about 35–40 minutes.

Turn out cake from the mold and let cool.

Mohr-im-Hemd Cake

Separate eggs. Melt couverture chocolate coating over steam. Stir soft butter with vanilla sugar, $1/3$ cup (60 g) granulated sugar, and salt until creamy. Gradually stir in egg yolks. Finally mix in the chocolate couverture.

Beat egg whites with remaining granulated sugar until stiff. Stir together $1/3$ of the egg whites with the chocolate mixture; carefully fold in remaining egg whites, bread crumbs, and hazelnuts.

Pour into a buttered mold sprinkled with sliced almonds, spread batter up to the edges (see illustration, p. 180), and bake cake in a preheated oven at 310°F (160°C) for about 1 hour. Turn out cake from the mold, let cool, cut into pieces, and serve with whipped cream.

see illustration, p. 180

Yields one cake with 10 slices

8 eggs
just under 1 ½ cup (140 g) dark chocolate couverture
½ cup plus
2 tbsp (140 g) soft butter at room temperature
1 tsp vanilla sugar
¾ cup (140 g) granulated sugar
salt
just over 1 cup (180 g) hazelnuts or walnuts, ground
1 cup (60 g) bread crumbs*
butter and sliced almonds for the mold
whipped cream for garnish

*Best are cake crumbs or grated *Biskottes*; alternatively bread crumbs can be used.

Anise Cake

Stir soft butter together with powdered and vanilla sugars and salt until creamy. Gradually stir in eggs. Mix flour with baking powder and anise. Stir flour mixture into the butter mixture.

Pour batter into a buttered mold sprinkled with sliced almonds, spread batter up to the edges (see illustration, p. 180), and bake cake in a preheated oven at 325°F (170°C) for about 55 minutes. Turn out cake from the mold, let cool, sprinkle with powdered sugar, and serve.

see illustration, p. 180

Yields one cake with 12 slices

1 heaping cup (250 g) soft butter at room temperature
just under
2 cups (250 g) powdered sugar
2 tsp vanilla sugar
salt
5 eggs
3 cups (300 g) flour (fine)
1 pinch of baking powder
3 tbsp (20 g) anise seed
butter and sliced almonds (or grated hazelnuts) for the mold
powdered sugar for sprinkling

Pear Cake

Yields one cake with 8 slices

Mürbteig:
1 ¼ cups (125 g) flour (fine)
¹/₃ cup (80 g) butter,
cut into small cubes
just under ¹/₃ cup (40 g)
powdered sugar
1 egg yolk
½ tsp vanilla sugar
peel of ¼ lemon (untreated),
zested
flour for preparing
²/₃ cup (120 g) raw marzipan
3 eggs
½ cup plus
2 tbsp (140 g) soft butter
a little over 1 cup (140 g)
powdered sugar
pinch of salt
1 tsp *Stollen* spice
(containing cardamom, orange
peel,
lemon peel, nutmeg, and
bourbon vanilla)
1 cup (100 g) flour (fine)
²/₃ cup (100 g) cornstarch just
under
¼ cup (20 g) cocoa
pinch of baking powder
3–4 stewed pears

Mürbteig: Knead all of the ingredients quickly into a *Mürbteig* dough; chill for at least 30 minutes; then roll out into a ¹/₁₀ inch (2 ½ mm) thick piece on a floured work surface or between sheets of parchment paper, then lift with the help of a rolling pin into a spring form pan (8 inches [20 cm] diameter) and spread it out inside. Cut off overhanging edges. Prick surface with a fork several times (= *stupfen*, so that the *Mürbteig* doesn't swell and rise irregularly).

Puree raw marzipan with one egg—preferably with a hand blender. Stir butter with powdered sugar, salt, and *Stollen* spices until frothy. Gradually stir in marzipan puree and remaining eggs. Sift flour with cornstarch, cocoa, and baking powder and gently fold into the butter mixture. Pour mixture onto the *Mürbteig* and smooth out.

Drain pears well, cut into fans, and distribute decoratively on the cake. Bake cake in preheated oven at 400°F (200°C) for about 50 minutes. Let cool and serve if desired with half-beaten, not-too-sweetened whipped cream.

Coconut Cake

Stir soft butter together with powdered and vanilla sugars, orange zest, and salt until creamy. Gradually stir in eggs and egg yolks. Fold in shredded coconut. Fold in flour and candied orange peel.

Pour into a buttered and floured mold, spread batter up to the edges (see illustration, p. 180), and bake cake in a preheated oven at 310°F (160°C) for about 1 hour. Turn cake out from the mold, let cool, bring orange marmalade to a boil, and coat the cake.

Yields one cake with 8–10 slices

²/₃ cup (150 g) soft butter at room temperature
1 cup (130 g) powdered sugar
1 tsp vanilla sugar
peel of 1 orange (untreated), zested
salt
4 eggs
1 egg yolk
2 ²/₃ cups (200 g) shredded coconut
½ cup (60 g) candied orange peel, chopped
¹/₃ cup plus
1 tbsp (40 g) flour (fine)
butter and flour for the pan

Date-Fig Cake

Wash figs in hot water, drain well, and cut into ¹/₅ inch (½ cm) cubes. Core dates and cut into ¹/₅ inch (½ cm) pieces. Mix figs and dates and sprinkle with brandy.

Separate eggs. Stir together butter at room temperature with powdered sugar, salt, cinnamon, and sugar until creamy. Gradually stir in egg yolks. Beat egg whites with granulated sugar until stiff. Stir together ½ of the egg whites and the dry fruit with the butter mixture, then fold in flour and remaining egg whites. Pour mixture into a buttered and floured mold, spread up to the edges (see illustration, p. 180), and bake cake in a preheated oven at 310°F (160°C) for about 1 hour. Turn out cake from the pan and let cool.

Tip: Vanilla ice cream or sweet cream taste wonderful with this cake.

Yields one cake with 10 slices

almost 1 cup (150 g) dried figs
1 cup (150 g) dried dates
3 tbsp brandy
5 eggs
⁷/₈ cup (200 g) soft butter at room temperature
just over ½ cup (70 g) powdered sugar
salt
1 pinch of cinnamon (ground)
1 tsp vanilla sugar
a little less than ½ cup (90 g) granulated sugar
just under 2 ¼ cups (220 g) flour (fine)
butter and flour for the pan

Fruit Bowls

Yields about 25 (2 inch (5 cm) diameter tartlet ramekins ½ inch (1.5 cm) high)

Mürbteig:
Half the quantity of the basic recipe (p. 165)

Vanilla Cream:
A quarter of the quantity of the recipe on p. 264
just over ¾ cup (80 g) dark chocolate couverture
variety of fresh fruits such as blueberries, raspberries, grapes, orange slices, etc.
1 package Torte jelly

Prepare half the quantity of the *Mürbteig* recipe (p. 165) as described.

Roll out *Mürbteig* $^1/_{10}$ inch (3 mm) thin between parchment paper; cut out pieces slightly larger than the tartlet molds and place them inside. Prick dough with a fork several times, bake in a preheated oven at 350°F (180°C) for 10–12 minutes until lightly brown and let cool.

Meanwhile prepare vanilla cream (p. 264), press through a sieve, and chill. Temper the chocolate and brush the *Mürbteig* bases with it (or use store-bought chocolate glaze). Fill vanilla cream into a pastry bag with a smooth tip and top the *Mürbteig* ramekins.

Wash and trim fruit, drain well, and place decoratively on the cream.

Prepare Torte jelly according to package directions and brush fruit with it.

Rehrücken

Yields one *Rehrücken* with 10
slices

5 eggs
1 cup (90 g) ground almonds,
1 ½ cups (150 g) flour (fine)
$^7/_8$ cup (90 g) dark chocolate
couverture
$^2/_3$ cup (150 g) butter
a little over $^1/_3$ cup (50 g)
powdered sugar
pinch of salt
1 tsp vanilla sugar
$^2/_3$ cup (120 g) granulated
sugar
butter and flour for the mold
4 ½ ounces (120 g) currant
jam

Glaze:
1 ½ heaping cup (300 g)
granulated sugar
2 ½ cups (250 g) dark chocolate couverture
whipped cream if desired

Separate eggs. Mix almonds with flour. Melt couverture chocolate coating over steam. Stir butter with powdered sugar, salt, melted couverture, and vanilla sugar until creamy. Gradually stir in egg yolks. Beat egg whites with granulated sugar until stiff. Stir together $^1/_3$ of the egg whites with the chocolate mixture; carefully fold in remaining egg whites with the flour-almond mixture.

Pour into a buttered and floured *Rehrücken* mold, spread up to the edges (see illustration, p. 180), and bake cake in a preheated oven at 325°F (170°C) for about 50 minutes. Turn out cake from the mold and let cool. Boil currant jam and evenly brush the *Rehrücken*.

Glaze: Bring ½ cup ($^1/_8$ l) water to a boil with sugar. Remove from heat. Break the couverture into pieces, add to sugar solution, and stir until completely melted. **Important:** Repeatedly brush off the rim of the pot with a wet brush so the chocolate does not burn. Heat glaze to 226°F (108°C) (thermometer or see tip) and strain into another dish. Pour about $^1/_3$ of the glaze onto a cold marble slab and spread with a spatula until the chocolate glaze has thickened (= so-called "tabling." See illustration, p. 265). In the meantime, gently stir remaining glaze every once in a while to prevent skin from forming. Brush the thickened glaze back into the pan and stir gently with the remaining glaze. Repeat this process until the entire glaze has thickened. Coat *Rehrücken* with glaze, let solidify, and serve *Rehrücken* with whipped cream.

Tip: The temperature of the glaze can best be checked by the so-called finger sample: First dip thumb and index finger in cold water, then in the glaze. Rub glaze between fingers. Open fingers: If the chocolate adheres in threads, the glaze is properly tempered.

Apricot Cake

Wash apricots, core, and cut into slices (depending on the size of apricots into quarters or sixths); dry well on paper towels.

Separate eggs. Stir yolks with ¼ cup (50 g) sugar until the sugar has dissolved completely. Stir soft butter, lemon zest, vanilla sugar, and salt until frothy. Gradually stir in egg yolk mixture. Mix flour with baking powder and sift. Beat egg whites with remaining granulated sugar until stiff. Stir in $1/3$ of each of the egg whites and the flour with a whisk into the mixture. Carefully mix in remaining egg whites and remaining flour.

Wrap a Torte ring (9.5 inches [24 cm] diameter) in paper or grease a spring form (9.5 inches [24 cm] diameter) with butter and sprinkle with flour. Pour $2/3$ of the cake batter into the form, smooth out, layer with wafers, and smooth remaining batter onto the wafers; place the apricot slices into the batter with the cut side up. Bake cake in preheated oven at 325°F (170°C) for about 1 hour.

Prepare jelly according to package directions and brush cake with it, remove cake from ring or spring form, and let cool.

Yields one cake with 12 slices

5 eggs
a little less than 1 cup (180 g) granulated sugar
peel of ½ lemon (untreated), zested
$1/3$ cup (80 g) butter
1 tsp vanilla sugar
pinch of salt
just over 1 ¾ cups (180 g) flour (fine)
½ tsp baking powder
¾ cup (300 ml) whipping cream
about 5 heaping cups (800 g) apricots
1 package Torte jelly
2 baking wafers

Pariserspitze

Yields about 25

Mürbteig:
$^1/_3$ of the basic recipe (p. 165)* flour for preparing

Paris Cream:
1 ¼ cup (300 g) whipping cream
3 cups (300 g) dark chocolate couverture
$^1/_3$ cup (80 g) hazelnut cream

Glaze:
3 cups (300 g) dark chocolate couverture
or compound coating (available at confectioner supply stores)

* Note: For this amount of tarts, you don't need the whole *Mürbteig*, but the dough turns out better when you prepare a larger amount. Leftovers can be wrapped in plastic wrap and frozen for several weeks.

Mürbteig: Prepare as described in the recipe (p. 165) and roll out on a floured surface about $^1/_{10}$ of an inch (3 mm) thick. Cut out dough circles (1 $^1/_8$ inch [3 cm] diameter) from the dough, place on a baking sheet lined with parchment paper, and bake in preheated oven at 400°F (200°C) for about 30 minutes until golden brown; let cool.

Paris Cream: Chop couverture chocolate into small pieces. Bring whipping cream to a boil, remove from heat, add chocolate, and stir until it is completely melted. Add the hazelnut cream and puree the mixture for about 1 minute with a hand blender. Subsequently pour into a shallow container and let sit; the cream should thicken, but not solidify.

Stir chocolate cream until smooth and top the *Mürbteig* bases using a pastry bag in the shape of a peak (smooth tip, about ½ inch [12 mm] in diameter); chill about 45 minutes.

Glaze: Prepare chocolate couverture or compound coating as described (p. 265) and dip the *Pariserspitze* with the tip down into the glaze and place on a wire rack. Serve in paper muffin cups.

A descriptive name, *Pariserspitze,* could be translated as "peaks of Paris."

Indians with Whipped Cream

Biskuit: Separate eggs. Stir yolks with salt, powdered, and vanilla sugars until fluffy. Sift together cornstarch and flour. Beat egg whites with granulated sugar until stiff. Stir together ¹/₃ of the egg whites with the yolk mixture, fold in remaining egg whites to the flour mixture. Fill mixture into a pastry bag with a smooth tip (²/₅–½ inch [10–12 mm] diameter) and top about 12 *Krapfen* on a baking sheet lined with parchment paper. Then bake in preheated oven at 400°F (200°C) for about 10 minutes. Wedge a wooden spoon handle in the oven door so it remains open a crack. Then finish baking *Krapfen* for about 10 minutes at 350°F (180°C).

Let *Krapfen* cool, detach from paper, and hollow out a bit with a sharp knife. Straighten half of the *Krapfen* on the bottom side so that they can stand well (these will be the bottoms of the *Krapfen*).

Glaze: Boil jam and dip the tops in the jam or brush them thinly with it; coarsely chop chocolate, melt over steam with fondant and a little water (it should thicken and reach a temperature of about 95–100°F [35–38°C]). **Note:** If fondant is too thick, dilute with water. Dip the coated tops in the chocolate fondant, drain, and place on a wire rack. Put the glaze in the preheated oven to dry for about 30 seconds at 140°F (60°C).

Filling: Before serving, beat whipping cream until stiff with sugar and pour into a pastry bag with a serrated tip. Put the bottoms of the *Indianer* into paper muffin cups, fill with whipped cream and place the glazed tops on top.

Yields 12

Biskuit:
5 eggs
pinch of salt
¼ cup (30 g) powdered sugar
½ tsp vanilla sugar
²/₃ cup (100 g) cornstarch
1 ¹/₈ cups of flour (fine)
½ cup minus
1 tbsp (80 g) granulated sugar

Glaze:
just under ½ cup (150 g) strained apricot jam
about ¾ heaping cup (80 g) chocolate
(with at least 60% cocoa content)
½ cup (150 g) fondant
a little over 2 cups
(½ l) whipping cream
powdered sugar to taste

In some cookbooks, these sweet pastries are known as Mohrenköpfe (Moors' Heads). Actually they should be called Inderkrapfen (Indian Krapfen): In 1820, an unknown confectioner dedicated them to an Indian magician who was currently triumphing at the Theater an der Wien in Vienna. The chocolate glaze was meant to evoke the artist's dark skin and the whipped cream, his dazzling white teeth. The magician has been forgotten, the confectioner never known: But the Indianerkrapfen, "Indians with Whipped Cream," became a popular dessert.

Cookies and Biscuits

Christmas was still a folkloric festival at the time of Maria Theresa, when the belief still lived on that the demons of the *Raunächte* (the "raw nights," the twelve nights after Christmas), who swept through the darkness between Christmas and Epiphany on a wild hunt, could be driven out with noise and good food. To placate them, you put honey pastries on the windowsill, and of course, whichever housewife made the best pastries had the best chance at putting the evil spirits of the winter night in a peaceful mood. Of course, the baked treats placed in the windows were actually gobbled up by children or pets. These usually weren't complicated Christmas cookies, but rather simple types of gingerbread.

They were sweetened either with honey or else not at all. If you leaf through old cookbooks, there are countless desserts that do entirely without sugar. The ancient culture of gingerbread is not least part of the history of honey. Nor did the tradition of Christmas baking derive from the confectioneries, but rather from the craft of the chandlers and gingerbread bakers.

However, truly refined pastries were rarely able to be conjured up with ingredients such as flour, nuts, and honey. Not until the *Biedermeier* period did cookbooks gradually fill with treats such as *Vanillekipferln* (vanilla crescents), *Witwenküssen* (widow's kisses), *Linzeraugen* (Linzer eyes), *Nussbusserln* (little nut kisses), *Florentinern, Mandelkissen* (almond pillows) . . . We owe this to the Prussian chemist Sigismund Markgraf, who made a discovery in 1747 that would make dessert history and liberate those of us with a sweet tooth. He found out that you can win sugar even from an ordinary beet and that sugar need not be produced as before only from sugarcane.

The universal dough for biscuits is the *Mürbteig* (shortcrust pastry dough). It can be differently shaped, seasoned, filled with jams or creams, glazed, or even simply sprinkled with sugar.

For all baked goods, the maxim applies: Weighing precisely is half the battle!

♦ *Mürbteig* succeeds perfectly if flour and sugar are finely sifted—the dough turns out very fine and homogeneous.

♦ Use cool butter but not too cold (but hands and work surface should be cold).

♦ Cut cool butter into small pieces or grate coarsely with a grater, crumble with flour, and knead quickly into a dough with the remaining ingredients.

♦ Whisk the eggs or yolk before mixing into the dough. The dough will turn out very smooth.

- Only knead the dough briefly, because the butter contained within must not melt—the dough would become crumbly and not formable. Or work the dough with the dough hook of a food processor: Add the ingredients to cool mixing bowls as rapidly as possible. Select the lowest setting and only stir briefly lest the dough become too warm.
- Wrap dough in plastic wrap and let it rest cool so that the butter within firms up again.
- Should the dough be crumbly or break during the rolling out, it can usually be saved by kneading in some egg white!

Parchment paper is a blessed invention: Especially delicate doughs can easily be rolled out flat and even between two sheets.

Basic Mürbteig Recipe

Briefly crumble flour with baking powder and butter between your palms. Stir together egg yolk with vanilla and powdered sugars, salt, and lemon zest and quickly knead into a *Mürbteig* with the crumbles; chill at least 30 minutes, then roll out $1/_{10}$ of an inch (3 mm) thick to baking sheet size on a floured work surface or between sheets of parchment paper. Place on a baking sheet lined with parchment paper, prick with a fork several times (so that the *Mürbteig* doesn't swell and rise irregularly). Bake in preheated oven at 350°F (180°C) for about 10 minutes until golden brown.

Yields 1 baking sheet

3 cups (300 g) flour (fine)
$7/_8$ cup (200 g) butter, cut into small cubes
heaping $2/_3$ cup (100 g) powdered sugar
1 pinch baking powder
1 egg yolk
1 tsp vanilla sugar
pinch of salt
peel of ½ lemon (untreated), zested
flour for preparing

Vanilla Kipferln

Yields 30

3 cups (300 g) flour (fine)
heaping ²/₃ cup (100 g) powdered sugar
1 egg yolk
1 tsp vanilla sugar
1 ¹/₈ cup (250 g) butter
2 ¹/₈ cups (180 g) walnuts,
ground
pinch of salt
1 pinch cinnamon (ground)
flour for preparing
vanilla sugar mixed with powdered sugar for tossing

Sift flour, stir together egg yolks with vanilla sugar, salt, and cinnamon. Cut butter into small cubes and coarsely knead together with flour. (Pieces of butter can still remain whole.) Add powdered sugar, walnuts, egg yolk mixture and knead into a smooth dough. Wrap dough in plastic wrap and chill for about 30 minutes.

Knead dough on lightly floured surface and divide into four equal portions. Shape each dough portions to form finger-thick rolls and cut into small slices. Shape slices into *Kipferln* (crescents). Place *Kipferln* onto a baking sheet lined with parchment paper and bake in a preheated oven at 350°F (180°C) for about 12 minutes. Let *Kipferln* cool briefly and toss in powdered sugar mixed with vanilla sugar.

Note: Sift vanilla-powdered sugar onto the baked vanilla *Kipferln* immediately, let cool, then sprinkle them again. This saves the step of rolling them in the vanilla-powdered sugar and the *Kipferln* don't break as easily.

Tip: Homemade vanilla sugar: 3 vanilla pods, just under 4 cups (500 g) powdered sugar (sifted). Cut vanilla pods lengthwise, place them with the powdered sugar into an airtight container and let stand several days.

Florentiner

Yields 40

just under ²/₃ cup (150 g)
whipping cream
¾ cup (150 g) granulated
sugar
1 tsp vanilla sugar
not quite ¹/₃ cup (100 g)
honey
peel of ¼ orange (untreated),
zested
1 cup (180 g) almonds
1 ½ cups (150 g) chocolate
couverture

Bring whipping cream to a boil with crystal and vanilla sugars, honey, and orange zest and boil at low heat for 1 minute (to about 230°F [110°C]). Stir in almonds, bring to a boil again, and remove from heat. Pour mixture onto a baking sheet lined with parchment paper and spread with a spatula. Place another sheet of parchment paper on the *Florentiner* batter and roll out to about ¹/₁₀ of an inch (3 mm) thick with a rolling pin. Remove top parchment paper and bake the almond mixture in a preheated oven at 275°F (140°C) until golden brown. Let cool about 5 minutes and cut into squares (1 ¹/₈ inch [3 cm] x1 ¹/₈ inch [3 cm]) with a knife; turn over using the parchment paper and then carefully peel it off; let *Florentiner* cool completely.

Prepare couverture according to the recipe on p. 265. Spread *Florentiner* with the dipping mixture and let the chocolate harden. Then, if desired, cut back the corners of the *Florentiner* and separate from one another.

Linzer Kipferln

Yields enough for teatime

3 ½ cups (350 g) flour (fine)
1 heaping cup (250 g) soft
butter
just over ²/₃ cup (90 g) powdered sugar
1 tsp vanilla sugar
peel of ¼ lemon (untreated),
zested
1 egg
just over ¾ cup (260 g) apricot
jam
1 cup (100 g) dark chocolate
couverture*

*Tip: Use ready-made chocolate
glaze.

Sift flour. Stir butter with powdered and vanilla sugars and lemon zest until creamy. Stir in egg. Last stir in the flour with a wooden spoon.

Fill batter into a pastry bag with a serrated tip (no. 7) and pipe onto a baking sheet lined with parchment paper in the form of arcs or crescents (about 1 ¹/₈–1 ½ inches [3–4 cm] in diameter); bake in a preheated oven at 350°F (180°C) for about 10–15 minutes until golden brown, remove from oven, and let cool completely. Fill jam into a small paper bag or disposable pastry bag, cut off the tip. Turn over half of the *Kipferln*, top with apricot jam, and stick these together with the remaining *Kipferln*. Melt couverture chocolate coating over steam and temper. Dip the ends of the crescents in the chocolate, let chocolate solidify.

Nusstaler

Nut Mürbteig: Stir egg together with vanilla sugar, cinnamon, and salt. Heap remaining ingredients on the work surface or in a food processor and knead with the mixed egg to a smooth nut *Mürbteig*. Roll dough into a flat brick, wrap in foil, and chill for about 30–60 minutes.

Filling: Bring ²/₃ cup (150 ml) of water to a boil with granulated sugar, honey, vanilla sugar, stir in walnuts, remove from heat, and add rum. Puree with a hand blender.

Roll out nut *Mürbteig* on floured surface about ¹/₁₀ of an inch (3 mm) thin, cut out cookies using a rosette cookie cutter (about 1 ½ inch [4 cm] in diameter), place on a baking sheet sprinkled with flour, and bake in a preheated oven at 350°F (180°C) for about 10–12 minutes until golden brown. Let cool. Stick together two *Taler* each with nut filling, then brush one side with hot apricot jam.

Chocolate Fondant: Warm all of the ingredients in a pot to 95–100°F (35–38°C). Dip the nut *Taler* with the jam side in the chocolate fondant, then immediately stick on a walnut half, and briefly dry in a preheated oven at 140°F (60°C) for ½ a minute (this will help maintain the gloss of the chocolate).

Tip: If the glaze is too hard, it can be diluted by adding water or rum. If it is too soft, add a little chocolate (chopped).

Yields about 70

Nut *Mürbteig*:
1 egg
1 tsp vanilla sugar
1 pinch of cinnamon (ground)
pinch of salt
5 cups of flour (fine)
2 cups of walnuts, ground
1 ¹/₃ cups of butter at room temperature
1 ¹/₈ cup (150 g) powdered sugar

Filling:
¾ cup (150 g) granulated sugar
not quite ½ cup (150 g) honey
1 tsp vanilla sugar
5 ¼ cups (450 g) walnuts, ground
2 tbsp (30 ml) rum
flour for preparing
apricot jam for spreading.

Chocolate Fondant:
¹/₃ cup (100 g) fondant
¹/₃ cup (30 g) chocolate, chopped
some rum water

Caramel Cookies

Yields 120

1 cup (200 g) granulated sugar
just under ½ cup (100 g)
whipping cream
6 tbsp (85 g) butter
not quite ¹/₃ cup (100 g)
honey
2 cups (200 g) almonds

Bring granulated sugar to a boil with whipping cream, butter, and honey, stir in almonds, and spread the mixture about ¹/₅ inch (5 mm) thick on parchment paper, cover with a second sheet of parchment paper, and roll out again with a rolling pin. This will help make the batter nice and even.

Let cool and cut into squares (1 ¹/₈ inch [3 cm] x 1 ¹/₈ inch [3 cm]). Place the squares into the 2-inch (5-cm) recesses of a silicone baking mat and bake in preheated oven at 295°F (145°C) for about 18–20 minutes until golden brown (not too dark!). **Tip:** If you don't have a silicone mold, prepare the batter like the *Florentiner* (see p. 168). Place the cookies in a *Rehrücken* mold while still warm (this gives them an "arc") and let cool completely.

Chocolate Krapferln

Yields about 70-80

Krapferln:
1 ⅛ cup (250 g) butter, room temperature
a little over 1 cup (140 g) powdered sugar
2 eggs
1 tsp vanilla sugar
pinch of salt
just under 2 cups (190 g) flour, sifted with
½ cup plus
1 tbsp (50 g) cocoa

Filling (Paris Cream):
1 ¼ cup (300 ml) whipping cream
3 ½ cups (350 g) couverture chocolate, chopped

Filling: Boil cream, add chocolate, and blend. Place in a shallow dish and chill. The mixture should not be completely solid; it should still be pourable and smooth.

Krapferln: Stir butter at room temperature with powdered sugar until very fluffy. Stir together eggs with vanilla sugar and salt and gradually stir into the butter mixture. Finally, carefully mix in the cocoa-flour.

Fill batter into a pastry bag with a fluted tip ($^1/_3$–$^2/_5$ inch [8–10 mm] diameter) and pipe *Krapferln* onto a baking sheet lined with parchment paper. Bake in preheated oven at 350°F (180°C) for about 10 minutes. Let cool completely.

Fill Paris cream filling into a pastry bag with a serrated tip and top ½ the quantity of *Krapferln*. Place the remaining *Krapferln* on top.

Tip: If desired, decorate with white chocolate and pistachios.

Spelt Almond Cookies

Yields about 70

1 cup (100 g) almonds
2 eggs
pinch of cinnamon (ground)
pinch of salt
1 ¹/₈ cup (250 g) butter
3 ¾ cups plus
2 tbsp (500 g) spelt whole
grain flour
¾ cup (150 g) whole cane
sugar

Coarsely grate almonds and roast in a preheated oven at 350°F (180°C) for about 7–8 minutes; repeatedly turn so the almonds are roasted evenly. Let cool completely.

Mix eggs and cinnamon with salt and knead with remaining ingredients into a smooth dough. Roll out dough between two sheets of parchment paper ¹/₁₀ of an inch (2–3 mm) thin. Remove upper paper, chill rolled dough for about 30 minutes.

Then cut dough into squares (1 ¹/₈ inch [3 cm] x 1 ¹/₈ inch [3 cm]). Using a spatula separate cookies slightly, place paper with cookies onto a baking sheet, and bake in a preheated oven at 350°F (180°C) for about 8–10 minutes.

Baking Test: When the cookies are slightly browned on the bottom, they are done.

Tip: Instead of almonds, you can also use hazelnuts.

Tortes

Tortes are the celebrities among pastries. Whenever they are served, you can almost hear the drum roll and fanfare.

Our idea of a classic Torte was solidified in the nineteenth century and shaped by the baroque; a rich, cream-filled structure of eggs, sugar, butter, egg whites, and little flour—a luxury product short on vitamins and long on calories.

What we call a Torte has undergone a certain development over the centuries, primarily as regards its taste. The word *Torte* is missing in medieval dictionaries; it appeared for the first time in 1418 and probably derives from the Italian "*torta*" (= round bread) and from the Medieval Latin "*Tortum*" (twisted bread). In French, "*Tourte*" means meat pie or oil cake, which also comes closer to the original execution of a Torte than our present-day Torte. In the medieval kitchen and during the renaissance, the Torte base was layered with meat and during Lent with fish. Old cookbooks are full of these Tortes that have more in common with meat pies. The filling was surrounded by dough, and then baked in a special pan or cake tin.

In the relevant cooking literature of the eighteenth century, recipes for sweet pies can be found for the first time, usually with artfully constructed decorations. Simple Torte rings made of tin were used to make them, the size of which could be adjusted at will; a kitchen utensil still worth purchasing today if you bake a lot of Tortes.

In the nineteenth century, a seemingly endless variety of Tortes developed. In addition to the traditional Tortes named for their dominant ingredient or method of baking, Tortes suddenly appeared bearing the names of their creators, such as *Dobos*, *Demel*, *Kofranek*, and *Pischinger* Tortes. Some of these delicacies were also named after their country or city of origin, such as *Linzer*, *Holländer*, *Mailänder*, *Traunkirchner*, or *Gmunden* Tortes, and sometimes persons from public life were the namesake, such as the *Esterhazy, Malakoff, Andrassy, Habsburg, Napoleon,* and *Kneipp* Tortes. In addition, there are also countless wedding, baptism, and other festive Tortes.

It's really not hard to become an exquisite Torte baker. All you need is patience, the necessary carefulness, and a few good ingredients, and nothing can really go wrong. There are no limits to the imagination when making Tortes.

The word *Torte* should not prevent you from experimenting with the form—they don't always have to be round! The same dough that solidifies into the familiar Torte shape in a spring form pan can also be baked in a loaf pan, resulting in a square cake that can be filled and glazed just the same. If you want, you can also cut square *Tortelettes* out of the loaf pan. For beginners in the fine art of Torte baking, this is often a lifeline.

The base is usually a foamy *Biskuit* cake, sometimes as is, sometimes prepared with nuts or chocolate. Not too heavy short crust pastries and, above all, crisp meringue crusts are worth layering. The question of which dough and which filling is a matter of taste.

If the Torte is to be glazed, it is recommended that it first be coated with a layer of hot jam. This makes the surface smooth and the glaze will not be absorbed by the cake. And of course, it's only the decoration that makes a Torte a masterpiece! That's why we artfully spray these baked goods with cream roses, creams, top it with homemade chocolate shavings, fresh berries, or marzipan fruits, with candied fruits, pralines, or mocha beans, you could continue this list endlessly. **Important:** Decorate as the whim takes you, and you will have a culinary work of art!

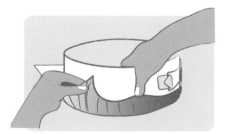

Basic Recipe
Biskuit Base

Biskuit Base: Mix flour with cornstarch and sift. Stir eggs with granulated and vanilla sugars, salt, and lemon zest until quite fluffy. Gently fold in flour mixture. Gently mix in hot butter.

Wrap a Torte ring (9.5 inches [24 cm] diameter) in paper (see illustration, p. 180) or grease a spring form (9.5 inches [24 cm] diameter) with butter and sprinkle with flour.

Pour in batter, spread to the top (see illustration, p. 180), and bake in a preheated oven at 350°F (180°C) for about 30 minutes.

Sprinkle Torte immediately after baking with flour or granulated sugar, cover with parchment paper, invert, and let cool completely. Then remove paper and continue working on the Torte according to the recipe.

Yields one Torte with 12 slices

¾ cup flour (fine)
¾ cup (80 g) cornstarch
5 eggs
²/₃ cup (120 g) granulated sugar
²/₃ tbsp (5 g) vanilla sugar
pinch of salt
peel of ¼ lemon (untreated), zested
¹/₃ cup (70 g) hot butter
butter and flour for the mold if desired
flour or granulated sugar for sprinkling

Strawberry Cream Torte

Yields one cake with 12 slices

Biskuit Base:
Half the quantity of the basic
recipe (p. 181)

Strawberry Cream:
about 5 sheets of gelatin
½ lb (250 g) strawberries
1 ⅛ cup (150 g) powdered
sugar
⅖ cup (100 g) lemon juice
1 ⅔ cup (400 g) whipping
cream

Decoration:
3 egg whites
⅔ cup (120 g) granulated
sugar
12 small strawberries, washed
and trimmed

Biskuit Base: Prepare according to the recipe on p. 181. Then remove paper and cut the Torte in half horizontally with a serrated knife.

Strawberry Cream: Soak gelatin in cold water. Wash and trim the strawberries and drain well, puree, and press through a sieve. Stir together strawberry puree with powdered sugar and lemon juice until smooth. Squeeze out gelatin well and dissolve over steam. Stir a little strawberry puree together with the dissolved gelatin, then mix well with the remaining strawberry puree; beat whipping cream not quite stiff, stir ⅓ in with the strawberry puree, carefully fold in remaining whipped cream.

Place a _Biskuit_ base in a Torte ring. Pour on half the amount of strawberry cream and smooth out; place the second _Biskuit_ base on top, press down gently, spread with remaining cream. Cover Torte with plastic wrap and refrigerate at least 2 hours.

Decoration: Beat egg whites with granulated sugar over steam (104°F [40°C]) until fluffy, remove from heat, and beat cold. Spread about ⅔ of the amount of egg whites evenly onto the Torte. Fill the remaining egg white mixture into a pastry bag with a serrated tip and pipe rosettes onto the Torte. Carefully flame the Torte with a blowtorch or Bunsen burner, decorate with strawberries.

Note: The decorative dabs on our photo give away a master pastry chef and are very difficult to achieve using regular household equipment.

Malakoff Torte

Torte Base:
Half the quantity of the basic *Biskuit* base recipe on p. 181

Biskotten:
5 eggs
2 ½ tbsp (30 g) granulated sugar
1 tsp vanilla sugar
pinch of salt about
1 ²/₃ cups (160 g) flour (fine)
powdered sugar for sprinkling

Cream:
4 sheets gelatin
¼ cup (¹/₁₆ l) milk
pinch of salt
¼ cup (¹/₁₆ l) strong coffee or instant coffee
1 egg yolk
¼ cup (50 g) granulated sugar
1 ½ cup (350 g) whipping cream

Rum Solution:
just under ¼ cup (50 ml) rum (38%)
a little over 1/₃ cup (50 g) powdered sugar

Decoration:
1 ²/₃ cup (400 g) whipping cream
a little powdered sugar
²/₃ cup (60 g) chocolate pistachios, chopped

Torte Base: Prepare *Biskuit* dough as described on p. 181. Cut out a disc from the dough (9.5 inches [24 cm] in diameter).

Biskotten: Separate eggs. Stir yolk with 2 tbsp granulated sugar, vanilla sugar, and salt until fluffy. Beat egg whites with remaining sugar until stiff. Stir ¹/₃ of the egg whites into the yolk mixture. Fold in the remaining egg whites with flour. Fill batter into a pastry bag with a smooth tip (¹/₃–²/₅ inch [8–10 mm] diameter) and pipe about 2 in (5 cm) long *Biskotten* onto a baking sheet lined with parchment paper. Sprinkle *Biskotten* with powdered sugar and bake in preheated oven at 410°F (205°C) for 8–10 minutes until they color slightly and detach from the paper, then remove from oven and allow to cool.

Cream: Soak gelatin in cold water. Bring milk with salt and coffee to a boil. Stir egg yolk with sugar until fluffy. Pour milk coffee into the yolk mixture, stirring constantly, and stir over low heat to a creamy consistency. Squeeze out gelatin well and dissolve in the warm coffee cream. Press cream through a sieve and chill until it begins to gel slightly. Whip cream until creamy; stir ¹/₃ into the cream mixture. Carefully fold in remaining whipped cream.

Solution: Bring just under ¼ cup (50 ml) of water to a boil with sugar and chill, add rum, and stir.

Place a *Biskuit* base in a Torte pan (9.5 inches [24 cm] diameter) and spread about ¹/₃ of the cream on it, layer with *Biskotten* (curved side down), brush these with the rum mixture, repeat (reserve 12 *Biskotten* for decorating), brush with rum mixture, and finish with cream.

Important: Work quickly, because the cream thickens rapidly. Cover Torte with plastic wrap and chill for at least 2–3 hours (preferably 1 day).

Decoration: Melt chocolate over steam. Dip the other *Biskotten* diagonally in the chocolate, put on parchment paper and allow to set in the refrigerator. Beat whipping cream with a little sugar (not too sweet) until stiff. Detach Torte from the edge of the Torte ring with a knife and remove it. Evenly spread ½ the amount of cream over the Torte. Fill the remaining cream into a pastry bag with a serrated tip and pipe rosettes onto the Torte. Top with chocolate *Biskotten* and serve.

The Malakoff Torte is among the classics of Austrian Tortes. It has its origin in Russia. During the Crimean War, the French marshal Jean J. Pelissier (1794–1864) stormed the Russian bastion "Malachov" at Sevastopol in the Crimea. For his spectacular success, he was knighted with the title of Duke. And since even in military circles sweet "sins" were enjoyed by all, a Torte was created for the occasion whose special feature was that it did not have to be baked.

Poppy Seed Torte

Yields one Torte with 12 slices

....

pinch of cinnamon (ground)
2 ½ tbsp (30 g) granulated
sugar
1 ²/₃ cup (220 g) poppy seeds,
ground*
just under ¾ cup (120 g)
hazelnuts, grated if desired
butter and
flour for the form
granulated sugar for sprinkling
4 ounces (100 g) currant jam

*The finer the poppy, the tastier
the Torte. The poppy should be
freshly ground, since ground
poppy seeds will go rancid quickly.
It is best to freeze ground poppy
seeds in a tightly closed container.

Separate eggs. Stir butter with powdered and vanilla sugars, salt, and cinnamon until frothy. Gradually stir in egg yolks. Beat egg whites with granulated sugar until stiff; stir egg whites together with the yolk mixture and fold in remaining egg whites with poppy seeds and hazelnuts. Wrap a Torte ring (9.5 inches [24 cm] diameter) in paper or aluminum foil (see illustration, p. 180) or grease a spring form (9.5 inches [24 cm] diameter) with butter and sprinkle with flour. Fill in batter, spread to the top, and bake in a preheated oven at 350°F (180°C) for about 50 minutes. Sprinkle Torte with granulated sugar, turn out onto Torte paper, and let cool. Then separate the Torte from the form using a knife and place it on a cake plate with the pretty side up.

Boil currant jam. Stir fondant with a little water and heat over steam (95–100°F [35–38°C]). Spread Torte first with jam, then with fondant. Sprinkle with chopped pistachios.

Variation: Prepare Torte with white poppies.

Tip: After spreading apricot jam on the Torte, you can also brush it with rum glaze (see recipe, p. 204).

Herren Torte with Punch

Separate eggs. Sift flour and mix with almonds and cinnamon. Stir yolks with 2 tbsp of granulated sugar, vanilla sugar, and salt until fluffy. Beat egg whites with remaining granulated sugar until stiff. Stir together $1/3$ of the egg whites with the yolk mixture. Carefully fold in remaining egg whites with almond flour.

Wrap a Torte ring in paper or aluminum foil (see illustration, p. 180) or grease a spring form (9.5 inches [24 cm] diameter) with butter and sprinkle with flour. Fill in batter, spread to the top, and bake in a preheated oven at 350°F (180°C) for about 35–40 minutes. Sprinkle Torte with granulated sugar, turn out, and let cool. Then separate the Torte from the mold using a knife and place it on a cake plate with the pretty side up. Wash Torte ring, dry well, and replace around the Torte.

For Soaking: Bring pineapple juice with sugar and 2 tbsp water to boil, remove from heat, and chill. Stir in rum and white wine. Brush over Torte base until all of the liquid is absorbed by the Torte. Beat whipping cream until stiff with a little sugar. Remove Torte ring.

Fill whipping cream into a pastry bag with a serrated tip and decorate the cake.

Yields one Torte with 12 slices

Nut Base:
5 eggs
2 cups (200 g) flour (fine)
80 g brown almonds or hazelnuts, grated
pinch of cinnamon
2 ½ tbsp (30 g) granulated sugar
1 tsp vanilla sugar
pinch of salt if desired
butter and flour for the pan

For Soaking:
$1/3$ cup (80 ml) pineapple juice
$1/3$ cup (60 g) granulated sugar
1 shot of rum
½ cup ($1/8$ l) white wine
granulated sugar
1 cup (¼ l) whipping cream
powdered sugar

Grillage Torte

Yields one Torte with 12 slices

Grillage Crumbs:
$^1/_3$ cup (60 g) hazelnuts (peeled)*
$^1/_3$ cup (60 g) granulated sugar

Grillage Batter:
1 cup (100 g) flour(fine)
¾ cup (60 g) walnuts, ground
6 eggs
¾ cup (140 g) granulated sugar
pinch of salt
pinch of cinnamon (ground)
1 tsp vanilla sugar
2 ¼ tbsp (30 g) oil butter and flour for the form if desired

Filling:
Half the quantity of the butter cream (recipe, p. 264)
4 cl (2-3 tbsp) brandy

Glaze:
about 3 cups (300 g) dark chocolate couverture
if desired, chocolate *Taler* coins for decoration

* To roast hazelnuts: Place hazelnuts on a baking sheet in a preheated oven at 350°F (180°C) and roast until the skin pops open. Let cool slightly. Wrap nuts in a clean kitchen cloth, and rub until the skin loosens.

Grillage Crumbs: Coarsely chop peeled hazelnuts. Slightly warm pan, melt sugar to a light caramel; remove from heat, mix in hazel nuts, and pour the caramel onto a lightly oiled baking sheet (or parchment paper); let cool. Crush, preferably with a mallet, and coarsely grate with a nut grater.

Grillage Batter: Mix flour, grated nuts, and *Grillage* crumbs. Separate eggs. Stir yolks $^1/_3$ of the granulated sugar, salt, cinnamon, 1 tablespoon water, and vanilla sugar until fluffy. Beat egg whites with remaining sugar until stiff. Stir $^1/_3$ of the egg whites into the yolk mixture. Fold in the remaining egg whites and flour-nut mixture. Stir in oil.

Wrap a Torte ring in paper (see illustration, p. 180) or grease a spring form (9.5 inches [24 cm] diameter) and sprinkle with flour. Pour in batter, bake in a preheated oven at 350°F (180°C) for about 45 minutes; let cool in the form.

Filling: Prepare recipe as described (p. 26) and stir with brandy until smooth.

Release Torte from the mold, cut with a serrated knife twice horizontally. Place a nut base in a Torte ring or a spring form, spread $^1/_3$ of the cream on the Torte base, lay a second base on top, and press down gently; spread another $^1/_3$ of the cream on top, put on the last base, and press down gently. Press down on Torte briefly with a not-too-heavy object. Refrigerate Torte for about 1 hour. Then detach Torte from the edge of the Torte ring with a knife and remove it. Spread remaining cream on the Torte and allow to set in the refrigerator for about 30 minutes.

Glaze: Prepare couverture as described on p. 265. Glaze the Torte and let glaze set.** Serve cake decorated with chocolate *Taler* coins.

**The Torte can also be made with the following glaze: Melt heaping ½ cup (120 g) butter (but not hot). Melt 1 1/3 cup (130 g) dark chocolate couverture over steam and stir together with the butter; let cool slightly and glaze the Torte completely.

Punch Torte

Biskuit

1 cup (100 g) flour(fine) about
$^2/_5$ cup (60 g) cornstarch
6 eggs
a little less than 1 cup
(180 g) granulated sugar
peel of ½ lemon
(untreated), zested
pinch of salt
$^1/_3$ cup (75 g) butter or ghee
butter and
flour for the forms if desired

Punch:

4 cl (2–3 tbsp) rum
$^1/_3$ cup (80 ml) water
a little less than ½ cup (90 g)
granulated sugar
peel of ½ orange (untreated),
zested
juice of 1 orange
2 tbsp apricot jams
about ¾ cup (250 g) apricot
jam
½ cup (150 g) fondant

Bake the *Biskuit* bases for the Torte the day before. Mix flour with cornstarch and sift. Separate eggs. Stir yolk with 2 tbsp granulated sugar, lemon zest, and salt until fluffy. Beat egg whites with remaining sugar until stiff. Stir $^1/_3$ of the egg whites in with the yolk mixture, carefully fold in remaining egg whites and flour. Melt butter and stir in while still hot.

Wrap two Torte rings in paper or aluminum foil (see illustration, p. 180) or grease two spring forms (9.5 inches [24 cm] diameter) with butter and sprinkle with flour. Fill ½ of the *Biskuit* batter into each of the prepared forms and bake in preheated oven at 350°F (180°C) for about 30 minutes; let cool.

Cut half a *Biskuit* in about $^1/_5$ inch (½ cm) cubes, drizzle with rum, and let stand. Bring water, sugar, orange zest, and juice to a boil and stir in apricot jam. Stir in *Biskuit* cubes and mix well with the liquid. **Note:** The *Biskuit* cubes should be soaked, but remain whole.

Cut the second *Biskuit* base horizontally with a serrated knife; spread both cut surfaces with about ½ the quantity of apricot jam. Place one of the bases in a Torte ring and evenly distribute the punch filling on it; if necessary, press down with your fingers at the edge. Put the second base on the filling, jam side down, and gently press down. Weigh down Torte with a flat object and chill for 2–3 hours. Remove Torte ring. Invert Torte and place on a Torte platter. Boil remaining jam and brush the Torte surface and edges with it. Warm fondant over steam while constantly stirring to about 95–100°F (35–38°C), stir with cherry brandy or pink food coloring until smooth and colored light pink. Quickly spread fondant as smoothly as possible onto the Torte surface using a spatula (**Note:** it should not flow over the edge) and immediately let dry in a preheated oven at 275°F (140°C) for about ½ a minute. Let Torte cool about 30 minutes. Sprinkle Torte edge with almonds (illustration).

Truffle Torte

Yields 1 Torte with 12 slices

Chocolate-Nut Base:
2 cups (200 g) dark chocolate
couverture
6 eggs
just under ¾ cup (70 g) flour
(fine)
1 ½ heaping cups (270 g)
hazelnuts, grated
⅞ cup (200 g) butter
just over ⅔ cup (90 g) powdered sugar
1 tsp vanilla sugar
pinch of salt
⅔ cup (120 g) granulated
sugar
if desired butter and flour for
the pan

Truffle Cream:
½ cup (1/8 l) whipping cream
4 cups (400 g) dark chocolate
couverture
3 tbsp rum
Chocolate shavings for garnish

Chocolate-Nut Base: Melt chocolate over steam. Separate eggs. Sift flour and mix with hazelnuts. Beat butter together with powdered and vanilla sugars and salt until creamy. Gradually stir in yolk, then fold in the melted chocolate. Beat egg whites with granulated sugar until stiff. Stir together ⅓ of the egg whites with the yolk mixture. Carefully fold in remaining egg whites with hazelnut flour.

Wrap a Torte ring in paper or aluminum foil (see illustration, p. 180) or grease a spring form (9.5 inches [24 cm] diameter) with butter and sprinkle with flour. Fill in batter, spread to the top, and bake in a preheated oven at 350°F (180°C) for about 1 hour. Let Torte cool, cut out of the ring, or remove from the mold. Cut Torte with a serrated knife twice horizontally so that three bases result.

Truffle Cream: Bring whipping cream to a boil, remove from heat, add chocolate, and stir until the chocolate is completely melted. Stir in rum. Chill cream and let set slightly.

Place a Torte base in a Torte ring. Spread ⅓ of the cream on it, cover with the second base, spread ⅓ of the cream on that one, and carefully press on the third base; cover Torte with foil and chill for about 2 hours.

Detach Torte from the edge of the Torte ring with a knife and remove it. Heat remaining cream over steam until it thickens, pour over the Torte, and brush the Torte evenly; sprinkle with chocolate shavings. **Note:** The cream still needs to be soft, otherwise the chocolate shavings won't stick. If the cream has set too much, place the Torte in a preheated oven for a few seconds at 215°F (100°C) or melt slightly with a blowtorch or Bunsen burner.

Williams Torte

Biskuit Base: Prepare according to the recipe on p. 181 and cut horizontally.

Poached Pears: Wash and peel pears and remove cores. Bring 1 cup (¼ l) water to a boil with sugar, lemon juice, and Williams brandy. Insert pears, cover, and cook until al dente; remove from heat and let cool in the broth.

Cream: Soak gelatin in plenty of cold water. Bring milk with vanilla sugar and salt to a boil. Stir yolks with sugar until smooth with a whisk. Pour boiling milk into the yolks and stir until the mixture is thick and creamy.

Squeeze out gelatin well and dissolve in the warm cream by stirring. Strain cream through a sieve or puree with a hand blender and refrigerate until it begins to thicken slightly. Then stir cream with Williams brandy until smooth. Whip cream until stiff. Stir ⅓ of the whipping cream into the cream mixture; carefully fold in remaining whipping cream.

Surround *Biskuit* base with a Torte ring. Remove ¼ of the pears from the broth, drain well, and dice. Distribute pear cubes on the *Biskuit* base. Spread cream (up to about 3 tablespoons) onto the pear cubes, distribute evenly, and cover with the second *Biskuit* base. Spread on remaining cream, cover with foil, and chill Torte for about 2 hours.

Remove the rest of the pears from the broth, drain well, and cut into thin slices. Cover Torte with pears in a fan shape. Prepare Torte jelly according to package directions and brush pears with it (= "glazing"): Then detach Torte from the edge of the Torte ring with a knife and remove the Torte ring (see illustration, p. 190).

Tip: The easy way to remove a Torte ring: Carefully warm the Torte rings from the outside with a blowtorch (Bunsen burner) and remove the ring.

Yields 1 Torte with 12 slices

Biskuit **Base:**
See recipe (p. 181)

Poached Pears:
1 ⅓ lbs (600 g) pears
(Bartlett)
½ cup minus
1 tbsp (80 g) granulated sugar
juice of 2 lemons
2 cl (1–2 tbsp) Williams brandy

Williams Cream:
4 sheets gelatin
½ cup (⅛ l) milk
1 tsp vanilla sugar
pinch of salt
1 egg yolk
⅓ cup (80 g) of granulated sugar
3 cl (2 tbsp) Williams brandy
1 ¼ cup (300 ml) whipping cream
1 package Torte jelly

Topfen Cream Torte

Yields 1 Torte with 12 slices

Torte Base:
Half the quantity of the basic
Biskuit base recipe (p. 181)

Topfen **Cream:**
5 sheets gelatin
1 cup (250 g) Topfen (20%
fat), strained
almost 1 cup (120 g) powdered sugar
pinch of salt
peel of ¼ lemon and ¼ orange (untreated), zested juice of
1 lemon
a little over ¾ cup (100 g)
sour cream
1 ²/₃ cup (400 ml) whipping
cream

Jelly Glaze:
¹/₃ cup (100 g) Torte jelly
just under ¼ cup (70 g) apricot
jam, strained

fruits and berries to decorate

Torte Base: Prepare ½ the quantity of *Biskuit* base as described (p. 181) and put in a Torte ring.

Topfen Cream: Soak gelatin in cold water. Stir together *Topfen*, powdered sugar, salt, orange and lemon zest, juice, and sour cream until smooth. Beat whipping cream until creamy. Squeeze out gelatin well and dissolve over steam. Stir in ¼ of the *Topfen* mixture; then stir in remaining *Topfen* mixture; finally, carefully fold in whipped cream.

Pour *Topfen* cream onto the Torte base in the Torte ring and smooth out the surface, cover with foil, and chill for about 2 hours—even better, freeze it.

Jelly Glaze: Prepare Torte jelly according to package directions. Stir apricot jam into the hot jelly, carefully pour over the Torte, and smooth out with a spatula; let set for a bit and remove the Torte ring.* Decorate Torte with fruit and berries.

* The easy way to remove a Torte ring: Carefully warm the Torte ring from the outside with a blowtorch (Bunsen burner) and remove the ring.

Wine Cream Torte

Yields 1 Torte with 12 slices

Biskuit Base: Mix flour with cornstarch and sift. Stir eggs with granulated and vanilla sugars, salt, and lemon zest until quite fluffy. Gently fold in flour mixture. Gently mix in hot butter.

Biskuit Base:
2/3 cup flour (fine)
2/3 cup (70 g) cornstarch
4 eggs
2/3 cup (120 g) granulated sugar
1 tsp vanilla sugar
pinch of salt
peel of ½ lemon (untreated), zested
just under
1/3 cup (60 g) hot butter
if desired, butter and flour for the form
granulated sugar for sprinkling

Wrap a Torte ring (9.5 inches [24 cm] diameter) in paper (see illustration, p. 180) or grease a spring form (9.5 inches [24 cm] diameter) with butter and sprinkle with flour.

Pour in batter, spread to the top (see illustration, p. 180) and bake in a preheated oven at 350°F (180°C) for about 30 minutes.

Sprinkle Torte immediately after baking with granulated sugar, cover with parchment paper, invert, and let cool completely. Cut *Biskuit* in half horizontally. **Note:** Only one *Biskuit* base is required, freeze the other wrapped in plastic wrap.

Wine Cream:
5 sheets of gelatin
1 2/3 cup (400 ml) whipping cream
½ cup (1/8 l) white wine (preferably Grüner Veltliner)
a little less than ½ cup (90 g) granulated sugar
4 egg yolks
juice and peel of ½ lemon (untreated), zested
1 tsp vanilla sugar

Wine Cream: Soak gelatin in cold water. Whip cream until stiff and chill. Stir together white wine with sugar, yolks, lemon juice and zest, vanilla sugar and beat over steam until frothy; dissolve squeezed gelatin in the warm mixture, removed from heat, and continue beating cream until it has cooled (= "beat cold"). Stir together 1/3 of the whipped cream with the cream; carefully fold in remaining whipped cream.

Decoration:
1 cup of whipping cream

Place Torte ring around Torte base, pour wine cream onto the Torte base, smooth out, cover with plastic wrap, and chill for about 2 hours. Beat whipping cream with powdered sugar until stiff. Cut Torte out of the ring with a knife or remove from the mold. Spread Torte with 1/3 of the whipped cream. Fill the remaining whipped cream into a pastry bag with a serrated tip and decorate the Torte. Top with decorative grapes.

Stirred Linzer Torte

Stir together milk with brandy and eggs. Sift flour with baking powder and mix with bread crumbs and walnuts.

Wrap a Torte ring (9.5 inches [24 cm] diameter) in paper (see illustration, p. 180) or grease a spring form (9.5 inches [24 cm] diameter) with butter and sprinkle with flour.

Stir together softened butter with powdered sugar, cornstarch, lemon zest, and vanilla sugar, a pinch of salt, cinnamon, and cloves until creamy. Alternate folding in eggs-milk and flour-crumb-nut mixture into the butter mixture. Pour in $1/3$ of the batter and smooth out. Cut baking wafers about ¾ inch (2 cm) smaller than the form and place on the poured batter. Evenly spread on currant jam.

Fill remaining Linzer batter into a pastry bag and pipe in a grid shape onto the jam. Pipe the edge of the Torte as well. Sprinkle Torte with almonds and bake in a preheated oven at 160°C (375°F) for about 1 hour. Let cool completely. Cut Torte out of the ring with a knife or remove from the form. Sprinkle lightly with sugar.

Note: The Torte tastes best when it is allowed to rest for 2–3 days in the refrigerator—covered with foil.

Yields 1 Torte with 12 slices

½ cup ($1/8$ l) milk
2–3 tbsp brandy or rum
3 eggs
1 ½ cups (150 g) of flour (fine)
tsp baking powder
1 heaping cup (100 g) of *Biskuit*, bread, or *Biskotten* crumbs
3 ½ cups (300 g) walnuts, ground
a heaping ¾ cup (180 g) butter at room temperature
1 $1/3$ cup (180 g) powdered sugar
2 tbsp cornstarch
peel of ½ lemon (untreated), zested
1 tsp vanilla sugar
pinch of salt
pinch of cinnamon (ground)
½ pinch of cloves
powdered sugar for sprinkling
butter
and flour for the form if desired

Lemon Torte

Yields 1 Torte with 12 slices

Biskuit:
¾ cup flour (fine)
²/₃ cup (60 g) cornstarch
4 eggs
²/₃ cup (120 g) granulated sugar
peel of ½ lemon (untreated), zested
pinch of salt
¼ cup (60 g) butter
butter and flour for the forms if desired

Lemon Cream:
1 cup (200 g) granulated sugar
1 ¹/₃ cup (300 g) butter juice and peel of 2 lemons (untreated), zested
2 eggs
2 tsp powdered sugar

For Frosting:
marzipan dark chocolate

Biskuit: Mix flour with cornstarch and sift. Separate eggs. Stir yolk with 2 tbsp granulated sugar, lemon zest, and salt until fluffy. Beat egg whites with remaining granulated sugar until stiff. Stir ¹/₃ of the egg whites into the yolk mixture. Carefully fold in remaining egg whites and flour.

Wrap a Torte ring in parchment paper (see illustration, p. 180) or grease a spring form (9.5 inches [24 cm] diameter) with butter and sprinkle with flour. Pour in *Biskuit* batter and bake in preheated oven at 350°F (180°C) for about 35 minutes; immediately sprinkle *Biskuit* with a little granulated sugar, cover with baking paper, invert so that it is on the sugared paper. Freeze *Biskuit* for 1 hour. **Note:** This helps the *Biskuit* to be easily cut into evenly thin bases.

Lemon Cream: Bring sugar to a boil with ⁷/₈ cup (200 g) butter, lemon juice and zest. Stir in eggs, return to a boil, and cook over low heat, stirring constantly, until the cream thickens. Press cream through a sieve and chill until it begins to set.

Cut *Biskuit* horizontally with a knife into 5 thin bases. Stir remaining (room temperature!) butter with powdered sugar until fluffy and gradually stir together with the lemon cream until smooth and creamy. Careful: The cream curdles easily!

Place a Torte base in a Torte ring and alternate lemon cream and remaining Torte bases, finishing with cream. Refrigerate Torte for about 1 hour. Then carefully cut out of the ring, smooth the edge of the Torte with a spatula, and frost with marzipan: Roll out the marzipan about ¹/₁₂ inch (2 mm) thin, frost the Torte with it (cut away over hanging pieces of marzipan with a dough scraper or a small knife), grate chocolate on top, place a piece of parchment paper on top, and rub it lightly using your palm (setting).

Chocolate Mousse Torte

Yields 1 Torte with 12 slices

Torte Base:

$^7/_8$ cup (90 g) dark chocolate
couverture
(at least 55–66% cocoa)
$^1/_3$ cup (80 g) butter
3 egg whites
2 tbsp (25 g) granulated sugar
2 egg yolks

Mousse:

½ cup (125 ml) whipping
cream
2 ¼ cups (220 g) dark chocolate couverture
(at least 55–66% cocoa)
4 egg yolks
1 $^1/_3$ cup (320 ml) whipping
cream, lightly beaten

Glaze:

See banana *Schnitten*, p. 224

Torte Base: Melt couverture with butter over steam. Beat egg whites with granulated sugar until stiff. Fold yolks and couverture into the egg whites.

Fill mixture into a Torte ring wrapped in paper (9.5 inches [24 cm] diameter) and smooth it out. Bake in preheated oven at 350°F (180°C) for about 18–20 minutes. Let cool, then remove paper and Torte ring.

Mousse: Boil cream and pour over the couverture, then puree with a hand blender and let cool to about 89–93°F (32–34°C) (= lip warm). Beat yolks hot over steam, then stir cold with a hand blender (until room temperature is reached) and quickly stir $^1/_3$ of this and $^1/_3$ of the lightly whipped cream into the batter. Carefully fold in the remaining yolk and whipped cream mixtures with a whisk.

Wrap Torte ring with plastic wrap, place on a Torte platter, insert Torte base, and pour on the chocolate mousse, then spread smooth. Refrigerate Torte at least 3–4 hours or freeze.

Glaze: Prepare the same way as for the banana *Schnitten* (p. 224). Place Torte on a rack, remove the ring and plastic wrap. Pour glaze over the Torte, smooth out with a spatula, and decorate if and as desired.

Cocoa Nut Torte

Yields 1 Torte with 12 slices

Nut Mixture:
just under 1 ¼ cup (120 g) flour (fine)
2 ⅛ cups (180 g) walnuts, finely grated
6 eggs
a little less than 1 cup (180 g) granulated sugar
2 tsp vanilla sugar
pinch of cinnamon (ground)
¼ cup (60 g) butter
if desired, butter and flour for the pan

Nut Cream:
¼ cup (50 g) sugar
1 ⅛ cup (100 g) walnuts, finely grated
2 tbsp rum
half the amount of the butter cream (p. 264)
cocoa powder for sprinkling
12 walnut halves for garnish

Nut Mixture: Sift flour and mix with nuts. Stir eggs with granulated and vanilla sugars and cinnamon until fluffy and the mixture no longer increases in volume. Gently fold in nut-flour mixture. Heat the butter and carefully stir in.

Wrap a Torte ring in paper 2 inch (5 cm) high or grease a spring form (9.5 inches [24 cm] diameter) and sprinkle with flour, fill in batter, spread to the top, and bake in a preheated oven at 350°F (180°C) for about 1 hour. Sprinkle Torte with sugar, cover with parchment paper, invert, and let cool; cut out of the ring or remove from the mold. Cut Torte with a serrated knife twice horizontally so that three bases result.

Nut Cream: Bring ¼ cup ($^1/_{16}$ l) water to a boil with sugar, add walnuts, and return to a boil, constantly stirring, remove from heat, stir in rum, puree with hand blender, and chill.

Prepare half the butter cream as described (p. 264). Stir $^1/_3$ of the butter cream together with the nut mixture; gently stir in remaining butter cream. Place a Torte base in a Torte ring. Spread $^1/_3$ of the cream on it, cover with the second base, spread $^1/_3$ of the cream on that one, and carefully press on the third base; cover Torte with foil and chill for about 1 hour. Cream should set so the Torte can be better brushed. Detach Torte from the edge of the Torte ring with a knife and remove it. Spread remaining nut cream on the Torte and allow to set in the refrigerator for 30 minutes. Mark portions on the Torte. Sprinkle Torte with cocoa. Using a pastry bag tip, make an indentation in each portion at the edge of the Torte. Fill the rest of the cream into a pastry bag with a serrated tip and pipe small dabs into these indentations. Decorate with walnut halves.

Note: The Torte turns out especially moist if the nut bases are soaked with rum mixture: Stir together just shy of 2 ¾ tbsp (40 ml) water with just under $^1/_3$ cup (40 g) powdered sugar and 2–3 tbsp rum and brush Torte bases with this.

Almond Torte

Mix flour with cornstarch and sift. Separate eggs. Stir yolks with vanilla sugar, salt, lemon zest, and raw marzipan paste until smooth. Add butter and stir until creamy.

Beat egg whites with granulated sugar until stiff. Stir $^1/_3$ of the egg whites into the marzipan mixture. Carefully fold in remaining egg whites and flour mixture.

Wrap a Torte ring in paper or aluminum foil (see illustration, p. 180) or grease a spring form (9.5 inches [24 cm] diameter) with butter and sprinkle with flour. Pour in batter, spread to the top (see illustration, p. 180), sprinkle with almonds, and bake in a preheated oven at 325°F (170°C) for about 1 hour.

Let Torte cool and cut out of the ring with a knife or remove from the mold. Sprinkle with powdered sugar and serve. Beat whipping cream with a little powdered sugar until creamy and serve with Torte.

Yields 1 Torte with 12 slices

1 cup flour (fine)
$^1/_3$ cup (50 g) cornstarch
6 eggs
1 tsp vanilla sugar
pinch of salt
peel of ½ lemon (untreated), zested
just under ½ cup (80 g) raw marzipan
a little over ½ cup (120 g) soft butter
½ cup (100 g) granulated sugar
¾ cup (60 g) almonds, sliced
butter and flour for the form
if desired powdered sugar for sprinkling
1 cup (¼ l) whipping cream

Ferchers Nut Torte

Mürbteig:
1 ¼ cups (125 g) flour (fine)
¹/₃ cup (80 g) butter, cut into small cubes
just under ¹/₃ cup (40 g) powdered sugar
1 egg yolk
1 tsp vanilla sugar
peel of ¼ lemon (untreated), zested
flour for preparing

Nut Mixture:
3 eggs
²/₃ cup (120 g) granulated sugar
1 ½ tbsp (15 g) cornstarch
1 tsp vanilla sugar
pinch of salt
1 ¾ cup (150 g) walnuts, ground
½ cup (30 g) fine bread crumbs
2/3 cup (140 g) melted butter

Glaze:
just under ¹/₃ cup (40 g) powdered sugar
²/₃ tbsp (10 ml) rum
about ¹/₃ cup (100 g) strained apricot jam

Place Torte ring or pie dish (9.5 inches [24 cm] diameter and 1 ¹/₈ inch [3 cm] high) on a baking sheet lined with parchment paper

Mürbteig: Knead all of the ingredients quickly into a *Mürbteig* dough; chill for at least 30 minutes. Roll out *Mürbteig* on floured surface about ¹/₁₂ inch (2 mm) thin and place in the Torte ring.

Nut Mixture: Stir eggs with granulated sugar, vanilla sugar, and salt until fluffy. Add walnuts with bread crumbs and butter (blend).

Immediately pour in nut mixture and slide the nut Torte into a preheated oven at 400°F (200°C). Reduce temperature to 350°F (175°C) and bake the Torte about 40 minutes. Carefully detach the *Mürbteig* from the mold with a non-serrated knife and briefly let Torte cool. Boil apricot jam and generously brush the Torte surface while still warm.

Glaze: Stir powdered sugar with rum till semi-liquid (95–100°F [35–38°C]) and brush Torte with it. Serve with whipped cream.

Caramel Cream Torte

Yields 1 Torte with 12 slices

Biskuit Base:
See recipe (p. 181)

Caramel Mixture:
a little over ²/₃ cup (160 ml) whipping cream
2 ¹/₃ tbsp (50 g) honey
½ tsp vanilla sugar
1 tbsp (15 g) butter
½ cup minus 1 tbsp (80 g) granulated sugar

Cream:
4 sheets of gelatin
1 ½ cup (350 ml) whipping cream
3 egg yolks
1 ²/₃ tbsp (20 g) sugar

Glaze:
1 sheet gelatin just under ½ cup (100 ml) whipping cream
1 tsp vanilla sugar for sprinkling
if desired, chocolate cookies for garnish

*Note: If only half of the baked Torte is needed, freeze the second half.

Biskuit Base: Prepare as described on p. 181. Cut base in half horizontally and freeze half if desired. Cut remaining Torte base in half again, resulting in two bases (½ inch [12 mm] each). Place a Torte base in a Torte ring (9.5 inches [24 cm] diameter).

Caramel Mixture: Heat whipping cream with honey, vanilla sugar, and butter, but do not boil. Melt sugar, pour the hot butter cream on top, and puree with hand blender until the caramel is completely melted, let cool. **Note:** Reserve ¹/₃ cup (100 g) for the glaze.

Cream: Soak gelatin in cold water. Lightly beat whipping cream. It should not be too stiff. Chill. Beat yolk warm over steam with sugar, remove from heat, and stir cold (keep stirring until cream is room temperature). Squeeze out gelatin well, dissolve over steam, and stir into the warm (about 89–91°F [32–33°C]) caramel mixture. Quickly stir in ¹/₃ of the whipped cream, then slowly stir in remaining whipped cream and frothy yolk with a whisk.

Put half of the cream on the Torte base in the ring, smooth out, place second *Biskuit* base on top, and gently press down. Spread remaining cream smoothly on top and refrigerate cake for about 2 hours.

Spread: Soak gelatin in cold water. Beat whipping cream with vanilla sugar until stiff. Smoothly spread onto Torte. Squeeze out gelatin well, dissolve over steam, and stir into the ¹/₃ cup (100 g) caramel; set aside. Once the caramel glaze starts to set slightly (slightly thickens), pour it over and spread to the edges using a spatula. Chill Torte about 30 minutes. Remove Torte ring (see tip**), cut Torte with a knife repeatedly dipped in hot water. Garnish with chocolate cookies if desired.

** Heat Torte ring with a blowtorch and carefully remove.

Schnitten and Roulades

"**A treat for the healthy,** often a necessity for the ill due to being nutritious and easy to digest and for one and all a companion for coffee or tea that is as pleasant as it is healthy." Thus reads the definition of *Biskuit* (sponge cake) in the *Appettit Lexicon* (Encyclopedia of Appetite) from 1894, a dish which has lost none of its popularity since then. This is perhaps because *Biskuit* is not a single dish, but rather a variety of baking batters that can be conjured into dozens, perhaps hundreds, of different of baked goods: Tortes, cakes, loaf cakes, Roulades—sweetly filled, but also *Omelets*, sweet *Stanitzel*, and *Petit Fours*—without *Biskuit* dough, the pastry kitchen would be poorer by quite a few attractions. It was not always thus.

The original form of *Biskuit* dough is the *Biskotte*. The ancient Romans had already invented this iron reserve for the packs of their legions, and simply baked them twice to help preserve them. Hence the name "*bis cotum*," meaning twice baked. "*Cotum*" became the Italian "*Biscotto*," whose preparation was first included in Austrian cookbooks in the seventeenth century. Thus we can find "*Bischgoten in a little paper house*" and "*Other types of Bischgoten*" in the *Garnet-Apple Cookbook* from 1699.

In French, word "*bis-cuit*" developed from *Biskotte*, which until the seventeenth century referred to a loaf of bread that was sliced and baked a second time for preservation until it was dry and crumbly. This *Zwey-back* (two bake) established itself as "*Zwieback*" (preserved bread for ships), and the "*Biskuit*" (also known as *Löffelbiskuit* [ladyfingers], *Kinderbiskuit* [children's sponge cake], or *Biskotte* in Austrian German) has become the epitome of a light pastry.

The transformation from hard cookie to light pastry did not happen without transitional stages: In the seventeenth century, the dough began to be refined using eggs, sugar, nuts, wine, and rose water. Not until hundred years later was the idea hit upon of separating the eggs and separately beating the egg whites and yolks until frothy before folding into the batter.

Important: All ingredients should be at room temperature. For the classic *Biskuit* batter, one egg per 2 ½ tbsp (30 g) of sugar and ¼ cup (20 g) of flour (fine). The higher the sugar content, the smaller the pores and denser the *Biskuit*. A low amount of sugar will make the dough very airy, but will also make it collapse more easily. The ratio of egg white to yolk can also be varied: Adding more yolks produces a drier, dark yellow sponge cake with fine pores. By increasing the proportion of egg whites, the dough comes out lighter, airier, and higher. There are two basic methods for introducing air to the batter: We distinguish between warm and cold beaten *Biskuit*:

With cold beaten *Biskuit*, either the egg whites are beaten with sugar until stiff and yolks and flour are then gently mixed in, or the yolk is stirred until frothy with sugar and spices (lemon zest and vanilla) and the flour and beaten egg whites gently mixed in.

With warm beaten *Biskuit* dough, the whole eggs are beaten with sugar over steam. This has the advantage that the sugar dissolves easily and the *Biskuit* turns out especially light and fine-pored. Important: The dough must not get too hot (water temperature about 120°F [50°C]).

The *Biskuit* dough must be baked immediately, since otherwise the incorporated air escapes and the *Biskuit* becomes hard. Don't neglect to preheat the oven. *Biskuit* Tortes and cakes are baked at about 350°F (180°C); cookies and biscuits at 400°F (200°C). Not on convection settings!

The dough is finished baking when the surface is dry and the *Biskuit* feels elastic to the touch. Let the dough cool completely after baking.

Zigeunerschnitten

Separate eggs. Melt couverture chocolate coating over steam. Stir butter with powdered and vanilla sugars until creamy. Stir in chocolate, gradually stir in egg yolks. Beat egg whites with granulated sugar until stiff. Stir together $1/3$ of the egg whites with the mixture; carefully fold in remaining egg whites and flour. Spread batter in the shape of a rectangle (16 inches [40 cm] x 12 inches [30 cm]) on a baking sheet lined with parchment paper and bake in a preheated oven at 400°F (200°C) about 12 minutes.

Note: During baking, wedge a wooden spoon between the oven door and the frame so it remains open a crack.

Then cut baked dough into 5 strips (3 inches [8 cm] x 12 inches [30 cm]) and detach from paper.

Paris Cream: Finely chop chocolate. Bring whipping cream to a boil, remove from heat, add couverture, and stir until it is completely melted. Let cream cool a little.

Once the cream has thickened a little but is not yet set, add butter and stir until frothy while drizzling in rum.

Stir raspberry jam until smooth. Brush onto 4 strips, then spread with cream. **Note:** Reserve a little cream for spreading on the surface. Stick slices together with cream and spread cream onto the surface of the slices smoothly and evenly.

Melt couverture chocolate coating over steam or temper (p. 265), glaze the *Zigeunerschnitten* with it, and sprinkle with pistachios.

Yields 12

5 eggs
½ cup (50 g) dark chocolate couverture
$1/3$ cup (80 g) soft butter at room temperature
a little over $1/3$ cup (50 g) powdered sugar
1 tsp vanilla sugar
½ cup minus
1 tbsp (80 g) granulated sugar
1 cup (100 g) flour (fine)

Paris Cream:
2 cups (200 g) dark chocolate couverture
½ cup ($1/8$ l) whipping cream
2 ¾ tbsp (40 g) soft butter at room temperature
2 cl (1–2 tbsp) rum

about $2/3$ cup (200 g) raspberry jam
2 cups (200 g) dark chocolate couverture
pistachios, coarsely chopped

Esterházyschnitten

Yields 10

¹/₃ cup (30 g) flour (fine)
just over 1 cup (180 g)
hazelnuts, grated
pinch of cinnamon (ground)
6 egg whites
¾ cup (150 g)
granulated sugar

Cream:
about 2 ½ cups (400 g) or
half the amount of
butter cream (p. 264)
about ¹/₃ cup (60 g)
hazelnuts, grated
1 tbsp brandy

Glaze:
just under ¹/₃ cup
(100 g) apricot jam,
strained
about ²/₃ cup (200 g)
fondant*
cocoa powder for coloring**

*Fondant is a concentrated su-
gar solution for glazing pastries
and commercially available.
**Instead of cocoa powder,
you can also use dark, melted
chocolate.

Esterházy Bases: Mix flour with hazelnuts and cinnamon. Beat egg whites with about ½ the quantity of granulated sugar until stiff, add remaining sugar, and beat. Fold flour-nut mixture into the egg whites.

Spread batter onto a baking sheet lined with parchment paper into a dough strip (14 inches [36 cm] x 16 inches [40 cm] long), smooth surface with a spatula, and bake in a preheated oven with top heat about 12 minutes until lightly browned. Cut dough while still hot into six strips (2 ¹/₃ inches [6 cm] x 16 inches [40 cm]) and allow to cool completely.

Cream: Prepare butter cream as described (p. 264). Briefly roast hazelnuts until they unfold their aroma; let cool and puree with brandy until creamy. Stir together nut mixture first with some butter cream, then with the remaining butter cream until smooth.

Spread each of the Esterházy strips with butter cream and stick together, placing the last base with the bottom side up. Chill for about 2 hours before glazing.

Glaze: Bring strained apricot jam to a boil and brush the surface with it. Stir fondant with a little water and heat over steam (95–100°F [35–38°C]). Stir together 3 tbsp of fondant with a little cocoa. Pour remaining fondant onto the surface of the slices and smooth out with a spatula (If the fondant is too set, use some water to achieve the desired consistency). Fill dark glaze into a disposable pastry bag (or paper bag), cut off about 1 mm from the tip with a pair of scissors; then pipe the dark glaze onto the still damp surface from a distance of ²/₅ inch (1 cm). Using a skewer, draw lines in the glaze. Let stand for another hour in a cool place before cutting. (**Note:** Not in the refrigerator, the glaze will dissolve there!).

Cremeschnitten

Yields about 10 *Schnitten*

about 1 lb (400 g)
store-bought *Blätterteig* or
basic recipe (p. 118)
flour for the baking sheet

Cream:
about 1 ¼ cup (200 g)
vanilla cream
(see recipe p. 264)
3 sheets gelatin
2 tsp powdered sugar
1 tbsp rum
2 tsp vanilla sugar
1 ²/₃ cup (400 g)
whipping cream
¼ cup (80 g) apricot jam

¾ cup (150 g)
granulated sugar

Roll out *Blätterteig* into a rectangle ¹/₁₂ inch (2 mm) thick (8 inches [20 cm] x 16 ½ inches [42 cm]), place a baking sheet sprinkled with flour, pierce with a fork several times. Then bake in preheated oven at 350°F (210 °C) for about 20 minutes (**Note:** The long baking time is important so that the *Blätterteig* gets crispy on the inside too!). Let *Blätterteig* cool.

Cream: Prepare vanilla cream according to recipe and let cool. Soak gelatin in plenty of cold water. Mix cold vanilla cream with powdered sugar, rum, and vanilla sugar. Whip cream until stiff. Squeeze out gelatin well and dissolve over steam. Stir together gelatin first with a few spoonfuls of the vanilla cream mix resolved, then quickly with the remaining cream and about ¹/₃ of the whipped cream until smooth. Fold in remaining whipped cream.

Cut *Blätterteig* into 2 equally sized pieces (8 inches [20 cm] x 3 ½ inches [9cm]). Brush one dough strip with cream and chill.

Place a second dough sheet onto a glazing rack and brush thinly with heated jam. Stir fondant with water until smooth and heat over steam. Pour onto the jam, quickly smooth out with a spatula, and let cool.

Cut glazed dough strips into 10 pieces with a sharp knife repeatedly dipped in hot water. Place remaining dough pieces close together on the cream. Cut cream slices (preferably with an electric knife) into pieces.

Note: You can brush the cream slices with sugar glaze instead of fondant. Stir powdered sugar with water and rum until thick, heat, and then glaze.

Yogurt Roulade

Biskuit: Sift flour. Stir yolk with salt, lemon zest, and $1/3$ of the granulated sugar until creamy and the mixture no longer increases in volume and the sugar is completely dissolved.

Beat egg whites with remaining sugar until stiff. Stir $1/3$ of the egg whites into the yolk mixture. Carefully fold in remaining egg whites and flour.

Spread batter in the shape of a rectangle (16 inches [40 cm] x 8 inches [20 cm]) on a baking sheet lined with parchment paper and bake in a preheated oven at 425°F (220°C) about 10–12 minutes. Sprinkle *Biskuit* with sugar, cover with parchment paper, invert, and let *Biskuit* cool thoroughly.

Cream: Soak gelatin in plenty of cold water. Stir yogurt with powdered sugar, lemon juice, and zest until smooth. Squeeze out gelatin well, dissolve over steam, and stir together with ¼ of the yogurt mixture. Beat whipping cream until stiff and fold into the remaining yogurt mixture.

Remove baked-on paper from the *Biskuit*. Spread on the cream so that it rises in the middle. Let set in the refrigerator. Roll up Roulade using paper and secure with a ruler (see illustration, p. 210). Place the Roulade with the closed paper side down on a platter, chill for at least 1 hour. Remove paper, cut the yogurt Roulade into about 1 $1/8$ inch (3 cm) thick slices, sprinkle with sugar, and serve garnished with strawberry halves.

Yields 1 Roulade with 10 pieces

Biskuit:
$2/3$ cup of flour (fine)
5 egg yolks
pinch of salt
peel of ¼ lemon (untreated), zested
½ cup minus
1 tbsp (80 g) granulated sugar
4 egg whites

granulated sugar

Cream:
6 sheets gelatin
4 $2/3$ cups (300 g) yogurt
just under $2/3$ cup (80 g) powdered sugar juice and peel of 1 lemon (untreated), zested
1 cup (¼ l) whipping cream

strawberries for garnish
powdered sugar for sprinkling

Kardinalschnitten

Yields 8-10 servings

Egg Whites Mixture:
5 egg whites
½ heaping cup (110 g)
granulated sugar
3 heaping tbsp (30 g)
cornstarch (wheat starch)

***Biskuit* Mixture:**
2 egg yolks
1 egg
2 ½ tbsp (30 g)
granulated sugar
½ tsp vanilla sugar
pinch of salt
$^1/_3$ cup plus
1 tbsp (40 g) flour (fine)

Coffee Cream:
1 ½ sheets gelatin
1 ¼ cup (300 ml) whipping
cream
1 tsp instant coffee
¾ cup (30 g)
powdered sugar

powdered sugar
for sprinkling

Egg Whites Mixture: Stir egg whites with granulated sugar and cornstarch until soft peaks form, fill into a pastry bag with a large smooth tip, and pipe two triple lines (about 4 ¾ inch [12 cm] wide, 12 inches [30 cm] long) onto a baking sheet lined with parchment paper at a distance of ½ inch (1 ½ cm).

Biskuit Mixture: Stir yolks with egg, sugar, vanilla sugar, and salt until fluffy, fold in flour. Fill the *Biskuit* mixture into a pastry bag with a large smooth tip and pipe evenly between the egg white lines. Sprinkle well with powdered sugar and bake in a preheated oven at 310°F (160°C) for about 30–35 minutes.

Note: Wedge a wooden spoon between the oven door and the frame so the door remains open a crack. Let the *Biskuit*-meringue strips cool, turn, and carefully remove baked-on paper.

Cream: Soak gelatin in plenty of cold water. Lightly beat whipping cream. Squeeze out soaked gelatin well, dissolve over steam, and stir together with instant coffee and powdered sugar. Stir $^1/_3$ of whipped cream in with the gelatin. Carefully fold in remaining whipped cream with a whisk.

Spread a *Biskuit*-meringue strip evenly with coffee cream. Place a second *Biskuit*-meringue strip quickly on top of the cream. **Note:** The two strips should align as exactly as possible. Refrigerate *Kardinalschnitten* for about 1 hour. Sprinkle with sugar and cut in portions.

Tip: Classic *Kardinalschnitten* are put together without cream, only using apricot or cranberry jam. In any case, well worth trying!

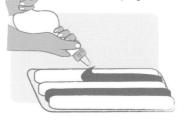

216

Pistachio Roulade

Yields 1 Roulade
with 10 pieces

Biskuit
4 eggs
$^2/_3$ cup minus
1 tbsp (60 g) flour (fine)
¼ cup (20 g) cocoa
½ cup (100 g) granulated
sugar

granulated sugar

Pistachio Cream:
4 sheets gelatin
½ cup ($^1/_8$ l) milk
1 tsp vanilla sugar
pinch of salt
1 egg yolk
¼ cup (50 g)
granulated sugar
1–2 tbsp maraschino ¼ cup
(30 g) pistachios
1 cup (¼ l)
whipping cream

flour for sprinkling
pistachios for decoration

Biskuit: Separate eggs. Mix flour with cocoa and sift. Stir yolks and $^1/_3$ of granulated sugar until creamy. Beat egg whites with remaining granulated sugar until stiff. Stir $^1/_3$ of the egg whites into the yolk mixture. Carefully fold in remaining egg whites and flour-cocoa mixture. Fill batter into a pastry bag fill and pipe onto a baking sheet lined with parchment paper (or spread evenly with a spatula), forming a rectangle (10 inches [25 cm] x 14 inches [35 cm]). Bake in preheated oven at 425°F (220°C) for about 12–15 minutes. Immediately sprinkle with flour, cover with parchment paper, invert, and let *Biskuit* cool thoroughly.

Pistachio Cream: Soak gelatin in cold water. Bring milk with vanilla sugar and salt to a boil. Stir yolks and sugar with a whisk until creamy, pour boiling hot milk into yolk cream, stirring constantly, and stir until the cream thickens. Squeeze out gelatin well and dissolve in the cream. Puree cream with a hand blender and chill. Puree maraschino, pistachios, and 3 tbsp of the slightly thickened cream with a hand blender so that the pistachio nuts are chopped. Stir cream with pistachio mixture until smooth. Whip cream until stiff and mix $^1/_3$ in with the pistachio cream. Fold in remaining whipped cream.

Remove paper from the *Biskuit*, spread pistachio cream on smoothly, chill, and let set. Then roll up Roulade tightly using the lower parchment paper sheet, wrap in paper, place on a platter with the closed paper side down, and chill for about 1 hour. Cut Roulade into portions, decorate with pistachios, and serve.

Rigó Jancischnitten

Yields 15

Chocolate *Biskuit*:
2 ¹⁄₃ tbsp (35 ml) milk
2 ¹⁄₃ tbsp (35 ml) oil
4 eggs
2 ½ tbsp (30 g)
granulated sugar
²⁄₃ tbsp (5 g) vanilla sugar
pinch of salt
just under 2 cups (190 g)
flour (fine) sifted with
¼ cup (20 g) cocoa powder
2 ½ tbsp (50 g) currant jam

Chocolate Cream
3 cups (300 g) chocolate
or couverture
chocolate
a littleover 2 cups (500 g)
whipping cream
5 egg yolks from
very fresh eggs
or 2/5 cup (100 g)
pasteurized egg yolks*
1 ²⁄₃ tbsp (20 g) sugar

Glaze:
1 cup (100 g) chocolate
or dark chocolate
couverture
a little under ¼ cup (50 g)
whipping cream

Cream:
just over 1 cup (250 g)
whipping cream
1 tsp vanilla sugar

*Available at confectioner or
restaurant wholesalers.

Line a baking sheet with parchment paper, place an expandable pastry frame on it and expand to 14 inches (36 cm) x 10 inches (25 cm). Warm milk with oil to about 130–140°F (55–60°C). Stir eggs with granulated and vanilla sugars and salt until quite fluffy. Fold in cocoa-flour and milk-oil mixture.

Add batter to the waiting pastry frame, smooth out with a spatula or dough scraper, and bake in a preheated oven at 410°F (205°C) for about 12–15 minutes; let cool completely. Then cut *Biskuit* from the pastry frame, turn over *Biskuit* base and pull off baked-on paper. Cut *Biskuit* into two strips (each 6 inches x 10 inches [15 cm x 25 cm].) Place a chocolate *Biskuit* strip onto a baking sheet lined with parchment paper, spread with currant jam, and surround with a pastry frame 6 inches x 10 inches (15 cm x 25 cm).

Chocolate Cream: Chop the chocolate coarsely and melt over steam (125°F [50°C]). Lightly whip cream and refrigerate. Beat yolk warm over steam with sugar, remove from heat, and then beat until cream is room temperature (= so-called beating cold). Stir ¹⁄₃ of the yolk mixture and the beaten cream quickly into the melted chocolate. Stir together remaining yolk mixture with the rest of the whipped cream, add chocolate mixture, and carefully mix. Spread chocolate cream onto the prepared *Biskuit* strip in the pastry frame, even out, and chill.

Invert the second chocolate *Biskuit* strip so that the "skinside" is on the bottom.

Glaze: Melt chocolate over steam, warm cream until lukewarm, pour into the chocolate, stir well, and then glaze the chocolate *Biskuit* strips with it, let set in the refrigerator. Cut into squares (2 inch [5 cm] length).

Cream: Beat whipping cream with vanilla sugar until stiff and distribute onto the chocolate cream in the pastry frame. (**Tip:** mixture can be filled into a pastry bag with a smooth tip and piped onto the chocolate cream) and smooth out. With a knife dipped in hot water, slide between cake edge and pastry frame and then remove the pastry frame.

Layer with glazed chocolate squares and cut into portion with a knife repeatedly dipped in hot water.

Rigó Janci is a Hungarian specialty cream Torte. It was named after the Hungarian Gypsy violinist Rigó, who was playing at the Cafe Gerbeaud in Budapest when Prince Joseph Chimay et de Carawan and his young American wife, Claire, were guests there. Claire and Janci fell head over heels in love, quietly left the cafe one after the other, and were never seen again.

Maraschino Roulade

Yields 1 Roulade
with 10 pieces

Biskuit:
See recipe (p. 210)

Cream:
3 sheets gelatin
a little over $2/3$ cup (160 ml) milk
2 egg yolks
3 $1/3$ tbsp (40 g) granulated sugar
1 cup (100 g) dark chocolate couverture, coarsely chopped
3 stewed pear halves

3 tbsp maraschino
powdered sugar for sprinkling

Bake *Biskuit* as described (p. 210) and let cool.

Cream: Soak gelatin in cold water. Bring milk with vanilla sugar and salt to a boil. Stir egg yolk with sugar until creamy. Pour boiling milk into the yolk mixture, stirring constantly, and keep stirring until the cream thickens. Squeeze out gelatin well, stir into the cream together with the chocolate, and dissolve. Press cream through a sieve and chill until it begins to set.

Layer an oval form or *Rehrücken* form with plastic wrap. Cut the cooled *Biskuit* so that it fits into the form and sticks out along the sides by about 1 ½ inch (4 cm). Then fill $1/3$ of the way up with cream. Drain stewed pears well, cut into wedges, and place on the cream. Cut off sections of the *Biskuit* and cover the pear wedges with it. Soak *Biskuit* with maraschino.

Spread on remaining cream, fold over overhanging *Biskuit* edges over the cream, and press gently into place. Cover with foil and refrigerate at least 2 hours to set.
Turn Roulade out of the form, remove foil, and cut the Roulade into about 1 $1/8$ inch (3 cm) wide slices. Sprinkle with powdered sugar and serve.

Nut Cream Roulade

Nut Biskuit: Separate eggs. Stir yolk with $1/3$ of the granulated sugar, vanilla sugar, and cinnamon until fluffy. Beat egg whites with remaining sugar until stiff. Stir $1/3$ of the egg whites into the yolk mixture. Carefully fold in remaining egg whites, walnuts, and flour. Fold in oil.

Spread batter smoothly onto a baking sheet lined with parchment paper; bake in a preheated oven at 410°F (210°C) for about 12–15 minutes. Sprinkle *Biskuit* with flour, cover with parchment paper, invert (so it is on the floured side), and let *Biskuit* cool thoroughly.

Nut Cream: Prepare butter cream as described (p. 264). Bring ¼ cup ($1/16$ l) water with sugar to a boil, add walnuts, and boil while stirring constantly. Remove from heat, stir in rum, puree mixture with a hand blender, and chill.

Stir $1/3$ of the butter cream with the nut mixture until smooth; then slowly stir in remaining butter cream. Remove baked-on paper from nut *Biskuit,* spread nut base with currant jam, apply cream evenly, reserving about 2 tbsp of the cream for decorating. Roll up Roulade (see illustration, p. 210) and chill for about 1 hour until the cream sets.

Mark portions on the Roulade. Fill cream that was set aside into a pastry bag, pipe small dabs onto the Roulade, and place 1 walnut half onto each dab of cream.

Yields 1 Roulade with 12 pieces

Nut *Biskuit*:
5 eggs
$2/3$ cup (120 g) granulated sugar
1 tsp vanilla sugar
pinch of cinnamon (ground)
1 cup (80 g) walnuts, ground
¾ cup (80 g) flour (fine)
$1/8$ cup (30 ml) oil
granulated sugar
flour for sprinkling

Nut Cream:
half the amount of the butter cream (p. 264)
¼ cup of granulated sugar
1 $1/8$ cups of walnuts, ground
2 tbsp rum

6 tbsp (120 g) currant jam
12 walnut halves for decoration

Bananenschnitten

Yields approximately 12

Biskuit:
7 eggs
²/₃ cup (120 g)
granulated sugar
1 tsp vanilla sugar
pinch of salt
1 ¹/₃ cup plus
1 tbsp (140 g) flour (fine)

Vanilla Butter Cream:
a little over 1 cup (250 ml)
milk
¼ cup (30 g) vanilla
pudding powder
1 tsp vanilla sugar
pinch of salt
½ cup (100 g)
granulated sugar
1 egg yolk
1 ¹/₃ cups (300 g) butter at
room temperature

just under ½ cup (100 ml)
of egg liqueur
about 3 lbs (1.3) kg
bananas

Glaze:
½ cup (¹/₈ l) whipping
cream
2 ¹/₃ tbsp (50 g) honey
1 ¹/₃ cup (130 g) dark
chocolate couverture,
chopped

Biskuit: Separate eggs. Stir yolks with 12 g of sugar, vanilla sugar, and salt until fluffy. Beat egg whites with remaining granulated sugar until soft peaks form. Stir ¹/₃ of the egg whites into the yolk mixture. Mix in flour and carefully fold in remaining egg whites. Spread batter in the shape of a rectangle (16 inches [40 cm] x 12 inches [30 cm]) on a baking sheet lined with parchment paper and bake in a preheated oven at 410°F (205°C) about 12 minutes. Then place a lightly floured sheet of parchment paper on top, invert *Biskuit,* and let cool.

Vanilla Butter Cream: Stir together milk with vanilla pudding powder, vanilla sugar, salt, granulated sugar, and egg yolks and bring to a boil while stirring constantly, cook over low heat until thick and creamy (stirring constantly). Remove from heat and stir cold. Gradually add butter while constantly stirring.

Remove baked-on paper from *Biskuit* and *Biskuit* in half width-wise; brush with half the quantity of egg liqueur and spread with about ¼ of the vanilla butter cream. Place second *Biskuit* half with the skin side down onto the cream, moisten with remaining egg liqueur, and spread with vanilla butter cream. Peel a banana, halve lengthwise, and place side by side on the cream. Spread on remaining vanilla butter cream and smooth out. Chill at least 2 hours—preferably overnight—so that it sets.

Glaze: Bring whipping cream to a boil with honey, add couverture, and gently stir and allow to cool to 86–90°F (30–32°C).*

Smooth out cold banana slices with a spatula dipped in hot water. Pour glaze onto the banana slices, smooth out, and briefly let set in the refrigerator. Cut into portions.

* Tip: If there are air bubbles in the glaze, knock the dish with the glaze several times on a work surface, then swirl.

Poppy Seed-Raspberry Schnitten

Yields about
15 servings

5 eggs
just over ½ cup (125 g)
butter at room temperature
just under ¹/₃ cup (40 g)
powdered sugar
1 tsp vanilla sugar
pinch of cinnamon (ground)
pinch of salt
½ cup (100 g)
granulated sugar
1 cup plus
1 tbsp (150 g) ground
gray poppy
½ heaping cup
(100 g) hazelnuts or
almonds, grated
¼ cup (25 g) flour (fine)
egg for brushing

½ cup (100 g)
soft butter almost
½ cup (60 g) powdered
sugar
tsp vanilla sugar
about 4 ⁷/₈ cups (600 g)
raspberries (can be frozen)

Torte jelly

Separate eggs. Stir soft butter with yolks, powdered and vanilla sugars, cinnamon, and salt until fluffy, beat egg whites with granulated sugar until soft peaks form and fold into the butter mixture. Mix poppy seeds with hazelnuts and flour and stir carefully into the mixture. Wrap a pastry frame (9.5 inches [24 cm] x 8 inches [20 cm]) or a Torte ring (9.5 inches [24 cm] diameter) in paper (see illustration, p. 180).

Fill batter into the prepared form, smooth surface, and bake in a preheated oven at 350°F (180°C) for about 30–35 minutes. Let cool in the frame or ring.

Stir softened butter with powdered and vanilla sugars until quite frothy, spread onto the poppy seed mixture, and even out. Top densely with raspberries. Prepare Torte jelly according to package directions and brush raspberries with it to glaze. Chill for at least 30 minutes. With a knife, slide along the pastry frame or Torte ring and detach the Torte jelly cake, remove frame. Cut into slices and serve.

Cream Desserts

About two hundred years ago, the well-known preacher Abraham a Sancta Clara spoke of "sweet dishes, sugared treats, crystalline jellies, tasty frolicks and bites of gold" as he enumerated all of the creamy, fruity, hot or cold dishes that crowned a meal.

Mousse is the noble description of the finest desserts, which literally melt on the tongue. In earlier times, these dishes were referred to simply as *Mus* (puree) or, in their sweet form, as egg cream. These exquisite dishes are also generally known as creams.

The base is always a very fine puree of fruits, nuts, milk products (such as yogurt, *Topfen*, or sour cream), often blended with whipped cream and gelatin.

Important tips:

♦ Gelatin has a natural "enemy," namely, the enzymes contained in tropical fruits like pineapple and kiwis, which split the protein and thereby prevent the gelatin from solidifying. Remedy: Blanch the fruits, thus rendering the enzymes inactive.

♦ When dissolving the gelatin, it is important that it first be soaked in cold water and then not heating too strongly while dissolving, preferably in a water bath or in hot (not boiling!) liquid.

♦ Important: Never add warm, dissolved gelatin to ice-cold liquid as it freezes suddenly and forms clumps.

6 gelatin sheets are sufficient to gelatinize 33 oz (1000 ml or 1000 g) of cream.

Chestnut Terrine

Yields 10 servings

Dark *Biskuit*:
5 eggs
1 tsp vanilla sugar
½ cup minus
1 tbsp (80 g) granulated
sugar
½ cup (50 g) flour (fine)
⅓ cup (30 g) cocoa
granulated sugar

Chestnut Cream:
7 sheets gelatin
1 cup (¼ l) milk
1 tsp vanilla sugar
pinch of salt
½ cup (100 g) granulated
sugar
a little over 2 cups (½ l)
cream
about 1 ¾ cup (250g)
chestnut puree (chestnut
rice)
2 tbsp rum

Rum Cream:
1 cup (¼ l) cream
1–2 tbsp rum
1 tsp vanilla sugar

chocolate shavings for
garnish

Dark *Biskuit*: Separate eggs. Stir egg yolk with vanilla sugar until creamy. Beat egg whites with granulated sugar until stiff and fold into the yolk mixture. Sift flour with cocoa and carefully fold in. Spread batter in the shape of a rectangle (10 inches [25 cm] x 12 inches [30 cm]) on a baking sheet lined with parchment paper, bake in a preheated oven at 400°F (200°C) about 12–15 minutes. Sprinkle *Biskuit* with sugar, cover with parchment paper, invert, and let cool.

Chestnut Cream: Soak gelatin in cold water. Bring milk with vanilla sugar and salt to a boil. Beat yolk with granulated sugar until frothy, pour milk into the yolk mix, stirring constantly. Cook over low heat while constantly stirring until creamy. Squeeze out gelatin well and dissolve in the warm cream. Puree cream, cover, and refrigerate until it begins to gel slightly. Stir 1 cup (150) g chestnut puree with rum until smooth. Beat whipping cream until creamy; stir ⅓ into the chestnut puree; carefully fold in remaining whipped cream. Pour chestnut mixture into a *Rehrücken* or terrine mold layered with plastic wrap.* Cut *Biskuit* so that the *Biskuit* base fits exactly on the shape of the cream-filled mold and covers the cream. Cover terrine with plastic wrap and let set in the refrigerator for at least 3–4 hours.

Turn terrine out of the form, remove foil. Pass the rest of the chestnut puree through a sieve, layer terrine with chestnut puree, and press lightly.

Rum Cream: Lightly beat whipping cream with rum and vanilla sugar. Cut terrine into slices with a non-serrated knife repeatedly dipped in cold water. Sprinkle with powdered sugar, decorate with chocolate shavings, and serve.

Tip: The terrine looks especially decorative when a finger-thick roll of chestnut puree is placed in the center (see photo).

*The correct way to layer *Rehrücken*, Terrine, or rectangular molds with plastic wrap: Press wrap firmly to the inside walls using a dishcloth; this way, no hollow spaces or air bubbles result.

Black Currant Cream

Yields 6 servings

Cream:
1 ²/₃ cups (250 g) black currants (can be frozen)
6 sheets gelatin
1 cup (¼ l) milk
½ cup (100 g) granulated sugar
1 egg
3 egg yolks
1 ¼ cup (300 ml) whipping cream
Juice of 1 lemon 2 oz Creme de Cassis (black currant liqueur)

Almond Foam:
just under ¼ cup (40 g) raw marzipan
½ cup (¹/₈ l) white wine
4 egg yolks
1 tbsp granulated sugar
2 cl almond liqueur (Amaretto)

Cream: Wash currants, remove stems, and bring to a boil with ½ cup (¹/₈ l) water; let frozen berries thaw. Then puree currants, return to a boil and strain through a sieve and chill. Soak gelatin in plenty of cold water. Bring milk and sugar to a boil. Mix eggs with egg yolks. Stir milk into the egg-yolk mixture, stirring constantly. Squeeze out gelatin well and dissolve in this. Strain cream through a sieve, and refrigerate until the cream slightly sets but doesn't thicken.

Beat whipping cream until creamy. Reserve 6 tbsp of currant puree for further processing. Stir remaining puree with lemon juice, crème de cassis, and ¹/₃ of the whipped cream with the cream base. Fold in remaining whipped cream. Fill cream into ramekins, cover with plastic wrap, and let set in the refrigerator for about 2–3 hours.

Almond Foam: Cut raw marzipan into pieces and blend smoothly together with white wine with a hand blender. Stir in egg yolks and sugar and add almond liqueur to marzipan mixture to taste. Just before serving, beat over steam until creamy.

Add a little powdered sugar to reserved currant puree to taste.

Take out ramekins from the refrigerator, remove wrap, and briefly submerge the ramekins in hot water. Turn out the cream onto cold plates, drizzle with currant puree, and serve with almond foam.

Yoghurt Cream with Berries

Wash berries, select the best ones, and depending on size, cut in halves or quarters. Small berries can be left whole. Mix $2/3$ of the berries with Bacardi and powdered sugar and let stand for about ½ hour. **Note:** Reserve remaining berries for decoration.

Soak gelatin in plenty of cold water. Stir yogurt with powdered sugar until smooth. Squeeze out gelatin well and heat it with the lemon juice. Stir some of the yogurt mixture in with the gelatin, then stir together with the remaining yogurt mixture. Beat whipping cream until creamy and fold into the yogurt cream. Distribute the marinated berries into glass dishes. Add cream, cover, and let set in the refrigerator for about 1 hour. Before serving, garnish with remaining berries and sprinkle with powdered sugar.

Tip: Instead of berries, other fruits such as cherries, mangoes, apricots, oranges, etc., can be used.

Yields 8 servings

about 1 lb (400 g) berries
(e.g., blueberries,
raspberries or strawberries)
3 cl (2 tbsp) Bacardi
powdered sugar

6 sheets gelatin
a little over 2 cups (½ l)
yogurt
almost 1 cup (120 g)
powdered sugar
juice of 2 lemons
1 ¼ cup (300 ml) whipping
cream

Grinzinger Wine Charlotte

Yields 10–12 servings

Biskotten:
See recipe (p. 184)

Wine Cream:
4 sheets gelatin
1 cup (¼ l) white wine
²/₃ cup (120 g) granulated sugar
juice of 1 lemons
3 egg yolks
1 ½ cup (350 ml) whipping cream

Currant Sauce:
2 ¼ cups (250 g) currants
almost 1 cup (120 g) powdered sugar
4 cl (2–3 tbsp) currant liqueur (cassis)

1 cup (150 g) seedless grapes for garnish.

Prepare *Biskotten* as described on p. 184.

Wine Cream: Soak gelatin in plenty of cold water. Bring white wine with sugar and lemon juice to a boil. Pour yolks into a bowl. Add wine stock to the yolks, stirring constantly, until creamy.

Squeeze out gelatin well and dissolve in the warm wine cream. Strain cream through a sieve and chill until the cream thickens slightly.

Beat whipping cream until creamy, stir together ¹/₃ of the whipped cream with the wine cream, carefully fold in remaining whipped cream. Pour wine cream into 10–12 ramekins or cups, smooth the surface, cover with foil, and let set in the refrigerator.

Currant Sauce: Wash currants, remove stems, bring to a boil with ²/₃ cup (150 ml) of water and powdered sugar, briefly puree (**Note:** the currant seeds should stay whole, otherwise the sauce will be bitter). Pass currant puree through a sieve, stir together with liqueur, and chill.

Wash grapes, remove stems, and drain well. Briefly dip ramekins hot water, turn out the cream, place on a plate, surround with *Biskotten*, carefully press down, and serve the Wine *Charlotte* garnished with grapes.

Orange Cream

Yields 8 servings

Yields 8 servings

3 seedless oranges
(untreated)
salt
7 tbsp granulated sugar
mint
or lemon balm, chopped
3 cl orange liqueur

Cream:
7 sheets gelatin
2 egg yolks heaping
$2/3$ cup (100 g) powdered
sugar
1 cup (¼ l) milk
1 tsp vanilla sugar

peel of ½ orange
(untreated), zested

Wash oranges. Zest peel of ½ orange and reserve for further processing (for the cream). Cut off peel of 2 oranges (best with a zester) and cut into thin strips. Bring orange strips (orange zest) to a boil in lightly salted water, strain, and wash in cold water. Then bring orange zest to a boil with ¼ cup ($1/16$ l) water and 3 tbsp granulated sugar, boil for 2 minutes; remove from the heat and let cool. Finish peeling oranges so that the white skin is also removed. Fillet oranges (cut out orange slices between the separation membranes with a small sharp knife). Drain orange slices on a wire rack well.

Mix orange slices with mint or lemon balm, mix remaining granulated sugar and orange liqueur, and let stand about 1 hour.

Cream: Soak gelatin in plenty of cold water. Stir egg yolk with sugar until frothy. Bring milk to a boil with vanilla sugar and orange zest and stir into the yolk mixture, stirring constantly; cook over low heat, stirring until creamy. Squeeze out gelatin well and dissolve in the cream. Strain cream through a sieve, and refrigerate until the cream slightly sets but doesn't thicken. Beat whipping cream until creamy. Stir orange liqueur into the cream. Stir in $1/3$ of the cream, fold in remaining whipped cream. Fill orange cream into ramekins, cover, and let set in the refrigerator for about 1–2 hours. Take out ramekins from the refrigerator, remove wrap, and briefly submerge the ramekins in hot water. Turn out cream onto cold plates. Arrange cream with orange segments, drizzle with the marinade, and serve garnished with orange zest and mint leaves.

Fried Apples with Cranberry Foam

Wash apples, remove cores. Slightly cut the peel of the apples multiple times with a knife. Wash raisins in hot water, drain well, and stir together with walnuts, cinnamon, and honey until smooth. Fill the apples with nut filling. Stir together wine with granulated and vanilla sugars and ½ cup (¹/₈ l) water and pour into a heat resistant pan or mold. Insert apples, brush with butter, pour over a little wine syrup, and bake in preheated oven at 350°F (180°C) for about 15–20 minutes until al dente. **Testing if done:** The apples should give a little resistance to piercing with a needle, but still be soft. **Note:** The exact cooking time depends on the size of apples.

Cranberry Foam: Stir yolk with sugar, apple juice, cranberry compote, vanilla sugar, and salt until smooth. Just before serving, beat cranberry mixture over steam until thick and frothy. Remove apples from the oven, let cool 5 minutes, and pour cranberry foam over half of them, serve immediately.

Yields 6 servings

6 red apples (preferably Jona Gold, russet)
²/₅ cup (60 g) raisins
not quite
1 ½ cups (120 g) walnuts, ground
pinch of cinnamon (ground)
3 tbsp honey
1 cup (¼ l) white wine
½ cup minus
1 tbsp (80 g) granulated sugar
1 tsp vanilla sugar
¼ cup (60 g) butter
for brushing

Cranberry Foam:
4 egg yolks
1 ²/₃ tbsp (20 g) granulated sugar
½ cup (¹/₈ l) apple juice
3-4 tbsp cranberry sauce
1 tsp vanilla sugar
pinch of salt

Coconut Cream with Poached Apricots

Coconut Cream:
6 sheets gelatin
4 egg yolks
¼ cup (50 g) granulated
sugar
1 cup (¼ l) milk
²/₃ cup (50 g) shredded
coconut
4 cl (2-3 tbsp) coconut
liqueur
²/₅ cup (40 g) chocolate
1 cup (¼ l) whipping cream

Poached Apricots:
a little over 1 lb
(450 g) apricots
¹/₃ cup (60 g)
granulated sugar
juice of 1 lemon
1 cinnamon stick
2 tbsp apricot liqueur

Soak gelatin in cold water. Stir egg yolk with sugar until frothy. Bring milk to a boil with shredded coconut, strain through a sieve, and pour into the yolk mixture, constantly stirring. Cook over low heat while constantly stirring until creamy. Squeeze out gelatin well and dissolve in the warm cream. Puree cream with a hand blender, cover, and refrigerate until it begins to gel slightly. Then add liqueur. Melt chocolate over steam. Beat whipping cream to a creamy consistency and fold in. Stir together ¹/₃ of the coconut cream with the melted chocolate. Fill remaining white coconut cream into ramekins; fill dark coconut cream into a pastry bag with a smooth tip and pipe into the center. Cover ramekins with plastic wrap and let set in the refrigerator for at least 2 hours.

Poached Apricots: Wash apricots, remove pits, and cut into quarters. Bring a little over ¹/₃ cup (90 ml) of water to a boil with sugar, lemon juice, and cinnamon stick, add apricots and apricot liqueur, and cook covered over low heat for about 1 minute. Remove from heat and let the apricots cool in the broth.

Remove ramekins from the refrigerator, dip briefly in hot water. Turn out coconut cream onto plates, arrange with apricots, drizzle coconut cream with the apricot broth, and serve.

Tip: This also tastes really good with apricot sauce. (See recipe, p. 258.)

Stuffed Pears

Yields 6 servings

6 medium ripe pears
(such as Bartlett or
Alexander)
½ cup (¹/₈ l) white wine
¾ cup (150 g) granulated
sugar
juice of 2 lemons
2 tbsp pear brandy
1 cinnamon stick or
cinnamon (ground)
3 level tsp cornstarch
¾ cup (75 g) chocolate,
coarsely grated
1 ½ cup (150 g) almonds,
coarsely grated
1 egg white butter
5 tbsp whipping cream

Bring wine to a boil with ¼ cup (¹/₁₆ l) water, sugar, lemon juice brandy, and cinnamon. Peel the pears (do not remove stems), carefully remove cores with a small spoon.

Place pears into the broth and cook until soft. Remove from the broth with a straining ladle and drain well. Reduce broth to about $1/3$ of the original quantity. Mix cornstarch with cold water, stir into the juice, and bring to a boil, constantly stirring; remove from the heat and let cool.

Mix chocolate with half the amount of almonds and fill the pears with it. Line a baking sheet or an ovenproof pan with aluminum foil and spread with butter. Brush pears with egg white, sprinkle with remaining almonds, and place on the sheet. Wrap pear stems with aluminum foil. Bake pears at 400°F (200°C) upper heat for about 10–15 minutes.

Whip cream until stiff. Stir the cooled pear cream until smooth and fold in the whipped cream. Remove aluminum foil from the pear stems and serve the pears with the cream immediately.

Strawberries in Riesling Jelly with Vanilla Cream

Wash and trim strawberries and drain well. Cut strawberries in half and place them evenly with the cut side down in glass bowls or shallow-stemmed glasses.

Jelly: Soak gelatin in cold water. Bring Riesling to a boil with sugar and lemon zest. Squeeze out gelatin well and dissolve in the Riesling. Stir in lemon juice, then strain through a sieve and flavor with orange liqueur. Chill. Once the jelly is set (but not yet thickened), pour over the strawberries and chill jelly 2–3 hours to thicken.

Vanilla Cream: Beat whipping cream with vanilla sugar until creamy. Serve strawberries in riesling jelly with vanilla cream.

Yields 6 servings

not quite 1 ½ lb (600 g) strawberries

Jelly:
5 sheets gelatin
a little over 2 cups (½ l) Riesling
1/3 cup (70 g) granulated sugar juice
peel of 1 lemon (untreated), zested
2 cl (1-2 tbsp) orange liqueur (Grand Marnier)

Vanilla Cream:
1 cup (¼ l) whipping cream
2 tsp vanilla sugar

Chocolate Mousse

Whip cream until creamy and refrigerate. Chop couverture into pieces and melt over steam (not above 104°F (40°C)!).

Stir together egg yolks, granulated and vanilla sugars and beat over steam until thick and creamy. **Note:** Keep rotating the mixing bowl and beat rapidly so that no lumps result. Remove mixing bowl from steam and keep beating until the cream is cold (= so-called "beating cold"). Quickly and firmly stir 1/3 of the whipping cream, chocolate, brandy, coffee, and 1/3 of the egg mixture together. Carefully stir in remaining whipping cream and remaining egg mixture. Fill glass bowls about ¼ of the way up with chocolate cream, cover with foil, and let set in the refrigerator at least 1 hour. Before serving, garnish cream with chocolate shavings and sprinkle with powdered sugar.

Yields 6 servings

not quite 2 cups (450 ml) whipping cream
1 ½ cup (150 g) dark chocolate couverture
1 egg
3 egg yolks
1 tbsp granulated sugar
1 tsp vanilla sugar
1 tbsp brandy
2 tbsp (30 ml) strong coffee

chocolate shaving for garnish
powdered sugar for sprinkling

Baked Figs

Biskuit:
5 eggs
1 tsp vanilla sugar
½ cup minus
1 tbsp (80 g) granulated
sugar
¾ cup (80 g) flour (fine)
granulated sugar

Currant Sauce:
See recipe (p. 258)

Basic Cream:
1 cup (¼ l) coffee cream
(15% fat)
3 ⅓ tbsp (40 g) granulated
sugar
1 tsp vanilla sugar
2 ¾ tbsp (40 g) butter
pinch of salt
about 1 tsp vanilla pudding
powder
2 egg yolks
3 cl (2 tbsp) almond
liqueur (Amaretto)
¼ cup (60 ml) whipping
cream

18 fresh figs
3 tbsp currant liqueur
(Creme de Cassis)
powdered sugar
for sprinkling

Biskuit: Separate eggs. Stir egg yolks with vanilla sugar until creamy. Beat egg whites with granulated sugar until stiff and fold into the yolk mixture. Stir in flour. Spread *Biskuit* batter in the shape of a rectangle (10 inches [25 cm] x 12 inches [30 cm]) on a baking sheet lined with parchment paper, bake in a preheated oven at 400°F (200°C) about 12–15 minutes. Sprinkle *Biskuit* with granulated sugar and cover with parchment paper. Invert *Biskuit* and let cool.

Prepare currant sauce as described on p. 258.

Basic Cream: Bring a little over ¾ cup ($^3/_{16}$ l) coffee cream with granulated and vanilla sugars, butter, and salt to a boil. Stir together remaining coffee cream with vanilla pudding powder and yolks until smooth, stir into the hot coffee cream, and bring to a boil while stirring constantly. Remove cream from the heat and—preferably with an electric mixer—stir until the cream has reached room temperature; cover with foil and refrigerate.

Remove baked-on parchment paper and cut out circles from the *Biskuit* (4 inches [10 cm] diameter), put on plates, and sprinkle with currant liqueur. Whip cream until stiff. Stir basic cream with almond liqueur until smooth, fold in whipped cream. Using a spoon, spread the cream evenly onto the *Biskuit* circles. The *Biskuit* circles should be entirely covered with cream.

Wash figs, gently pull off the skin. Cut figs in sixths, place onto the cream with the cut surface up, and sprinkle with powdered sugar. Wipe plate edges with a damp cloth or clean paper towel so that nothing can burn during browning. Bake plates in a preheated oven at 500°F (250°C) (broil) until golden brown.

Serve baked fig tarts with currant sauce immediately.

Parfaits

Even if the Italians do not want to hear it: they didn't invent this chilled delight. three thousand years ago, the Chinese were already blending snow with fruit. If legends are to be believed, Confucius (551–479 BC) used to interrupt his conversations with pleasant breaks during which he sipped iced fruit stored in man-high jugs in his ice cellar.

Greeks and Romans had snow and ice brought from Mount Olympus in order to enjoy a mixture of honey, snow, violets, rose water, and fruit juice as a refreshing dessert after meals. They also hoarded ice in cellars and well-covered holes in the ground to keep wine cool and meat fresh. This always reminds me of my father's stories, who had refrigerators in his tavern that actually drew their cold from blocks of ice. They were brought to the house by the iceman, carried on his shoulder in a coarse sack that protected from the worst of the cold. The block was then smashed into two or three pieces so it would fit in the refrigerator.

Ice cream, enriched with cream, was reportedly invented by a Tuscan and brought to Paris by Catherine de Medici. But the ice cream–loving Italians didn't leave it at that. Only once the Sicilian Procopio Coltelli began selling the first generally available ice cream in Paris across from the Comedie Francaise in 1662—with the permission of the king, the democratization of the feudal enjoyment began. People from across Europe traveled there to treat themselves to the frozen seduction. Even Marie Antoinette and her circle of courtly ladies supposedly enjoyed spooning out ice cream scoops as large as her fist from the cups at the Parisian Café Procope. As chroniclers reported, the fine ladies preferred licking up the ice cream with their tongues instead of using the intended spoons. One can only imagine what a provocation this caused! Very soon that certain café became the favorite target of many a gallant Parisian gentleman! Marie Antoinette's stern mother, Maria Theresa, had no patience for such "below-zero antics" and made sure the propriety of public ice cream slurping was closely monitored by the chastity commission she created . . . until Harry Bust from Ohio turned the Popsicle into good business and registered a patent for ice cream on a stick in 1923.

Parfaits are made of yolks or whole eggs, sugar, whipped cream, and the desired ingredients for flavor (fruits, chocolate, etc.). The batter of eggs and/or yolks is whisked with sugar over steam until it is warm and bright yellow. Due to the heat, the batter becomes very fine-pored, but the warmth also poses the problem that it can cause the eggs to thicken. Preventing this requires the batter to remain in constant motion, then removed from the heat and—preferably with an electric mixer—cooled to room temperature, i.e., beaten cold.

Then the other ingredients are stirred in, with the last ingredients always whipped cream and egg whites. Parfaits should always be thawed before serving for 10 minutes at room temperature. A previously thawed Parfait should not be re-frozen because bacteria multiply rapidly due to the interruption of the freezing chain.

Parfaits should always be frozen in closed containers or covered with foil, otherwise they dry out and lose flavor.

The Byzantines made their icy "*Sherbats*" from refined fruit mixes. These have survived as **sorbets,** that is, flavored water ice, and usually served in top restaurants as a palate cleanser between courses. I like sorbet as a low-calorie refreshment before or instead of dessert or a cheese course.

During the freezing process, sorbets must be stirred frequently so that the ice crystals do not become too large and the puree becomes smoother.

In southern Italy, the spooning out of *Granita* (a semi-frozen dessert similar to sorbet) is part of the daily *Dolce Vita*. In Sicily, in the summer there is even a granita di caffe at the breakfast table. The Sicilians complement them with traditional *Manuzza*, a loaf of bread in the form of a small hand.

Granitas are made from the same ingredients as sorbets, but with lower sugar content; in a low-sugar solution, small ice crystals form during freezing, which can then be scraped off as fine snow.

Tip: Only pour a little under ½ an inch (1 cm) of the mixture into the mold to speed the freezing process, which takes about 5 hours.

Coconut Parfait with Poached Peaches

Coconut Parfait: Pour shredded coconut on a baking sheet and roast in preheated oven at 400°F (200°C) until light brown. Immediately remove shredded coconut from the baking sheet and let cool.

Note: The shredded coconut would continue to brown on the hot sheet.

Whip cream until creamy and refrigerate. Stir eggs with yolks, granulated and vanilla sugars, and salt in a mixing bowl and beat over steam to a creamy consistency with a whisk, all the while rotating the mixing bowl and beating rapidly so that no lumps form. Remove mixing bowl from heat once the cream is hot, "beat cold" (beat until the mixture is cooled to room temperature). Then stir $1/3$ of the whipping cream with the shredded coconut in with the egg mixture. Carefully fold in remaining whipped cream into the cream. Pour into a *Rehrücken* form or terrine mold lined with plastic wrap, smooth out the surface, cover with foil, and freeze for at least 6 hours. Briefly dip the parfait in hot water, turn it out from the mold, and cut into slices. Place the parfait on chilled plates with peach wedges and, if desired, garnish with currants.

Poached Peaches: Briefly submerge peaches in boiling water, immerse in ice water, and peel with a small sharp knife. Bring ¼ cup (60 ml) of water to a boil with granulated and vanilla sugars and lemon juice. Halve peaches, remove pits, and cut into wedges. Place peach wedges into the broth and cook until al dente.

Variation: You can also remove $1/3$ of the peaches from the broth, puree them, and place the remaining whole peach wedges into the puree.

Yields 8 servings

Coconut Parfait:
1 ⅓ cup (100 g) shredded coconut
a little over 2 cups (½ l) whipping cream
3 eggs
4 egg yolks
1 cup (200 g) granulated sugar
1 tsp vanilla sugar
pinch of salt

Poached Peaches:
not quite 1 ½ lb (600 g) peaches
1 tsp vanilla sugar
¾ cup (150 g) granulated sugar
juice of 1 lemon

if desired, currants for garnish

Plum Parfait

Filling: Wash prunes in hot water, drain well, and place in a bowl. Bring 5 tbsp water and sugar to a boil, pour over the prunes with the plum brandy; cover with foil and let stand for at least ½ day. Subsequently, remove prunes from the marinade and drain well.

Plum Parfait: Whip cream until creamy and refrigerate. Stir eggs with yolks, granulated and vanilla sugars, plum brandy, and salt in a mixing bowl and beat over steam to a creamy consistency, all the while rotating the mixing bowl and beating rapidly so that no lumps form. Remove mixing bowl from heat once the cream is hot, "beat cold" (beat until the mixture is cooled to room temperature). Then stir $1/3$ of the whipped cream firmly into the egg mixture. Carefully fold in remaining whipped cream into the cream. Pour mixture into a *Rehrücken* form or terrine mold lined with plastic wrap, and push one prune into the parfait mixture. Smooth out the surface, cover with foil, and freeze at least 6 hours. Briefly dip the parfait in hot water, turn it out from the mold, and cut into slices. Place parfait on chilled plates, serve with plum sauce, and garnish with plum slices and pistachios.

Plum Sauce: Wash plums; remove pits, cut into large pieces. Bring 5 tbsp water to a boil with lemon juice, sugar, and cinnamon stick, add plum slices and cook until soft. Remove cinnamon stick. Puree plums, strain through a sieve, and stir in plum brandy.

Pistachio Parfait with Maraschino Cream

Yields 8 servings

Pistachio Parfait:
a little over 2 cups (½ l)
whipping cream
3 eggs
4 egg yolks a little less
than 1 cup (180 g)
granulated sugar
1 tsp vanilla sugar
2 tbsp maraschino
pinch of salt
1 cup (120 g) pistachios,
grated

Maraschino Cream:
1 cup (¼ l) whipping cream
2 cl (1-2 tbsp) maraschino
1 tsp vanilla sugar

Pistachio Parfait: Whip cream until creamy and refrigerate. Stir eggs with yolks, granulated and vanilla sugars, maraschino, and salt in a mixing bowl and beat over steam to a creamy consistency, all the while rotating the mixing bowl and beating rapidly so that no lumps form. Remove mixing bowl from heat once the cream is hot, "beat cold" (beat until the mixture is cooled to room temperature). Then stir $1/3$ of the whipping cream with the pistachios firmly into the egg mixture. Carefully fold in remaining whipped cream into the cream. Pour the mixture into small molds and freeze covered with foil for at least 6 hours.

Maraschino Cream: Beat whipping cream with maraschino and vanilla sugar just before serving into a thick cream. Turn out pistachio parfait onto plates (briefly dip molds in hot water, then the parfait will come right out of the molds) and serve with maraschino cream.

Chocolate Parfait with Red Wine Sour Cherries

Parfait: Bring ½ cup (¹/₈ l) water to a boil with cocoa; remove from heat. Coarsely chop couverture and melt in the cocoa. Stir in rum and puree briefly with a hand blender, then refrigerate.

Whip cream until creamy and refrigerate. Stir eggs with yolks, granulated and vanilla sugars, and salt in a mixing bowl and beat over steam to a creamy consistency, all the while rotating the mixing bowl and beating rapidly so that no lumps form. Remove mixing bowl from heat once the cream is hot, "beat cold" (beat until the mixture is cooled to room temperature). Then stir together ¹/₃ of the whipped cream with the egg mixture and the chocolate. Carefully fold remaining whipped cream into the cream. Pour the mixture into small molds and freeze covered with foil for at least 6 hours.

Red Wine Sour Cherries: Stir cornstarch in a little red wine until smooth. Bring remaining red wine to a boil with sugar and cinnamon stick, stir in starch, and boil at low heat until the sauce thickens. Drain cherries well and add. Sweeten if desired and let cool slightly.

Turn out chocolate parfait onto plates, garnish with lukewarm red wine cherries, and decorate with chocolate shavings.

Yields 8 servings

Chocolate Parfait:
½ cup (40 g) cocoa
just under
²/₃ cup (60 g) dark
chocolate couverture
or chocolate (at least 60%
cocoa)
2 tbsp rum
a little over 2 cups (½ l)
whipping cream
3 eggs
4 egg yolks
¾ cup (150 g) granulated
sugar
1 tsp vanilla sugar
pinch of salt

Red Wine Sour Cherries:
2 tsp cornstarch
1 cup (¼ l) red wine
¹/₃ cup (60 g) granulated
sugar
1 cinnamon stick
1 lb (400 g) cherry
compote
chocolate shavings for
garnish

Strawberry Yogurt Parfait

Yields 8 servings

1 cup (150 g) strawberries
juice of ½ lemon
1 ⅞ cup (120 g)
yogurt (3.6% fat)
1 ½ cup (350 ml) whipping
cream
3 eggs
4 egg yolks
a little less than 1 cup (180
g) granulated sugar
1 tsp vanilla sugar
pinch of salt

Yogurt Sauce:
1 ⅞ cup (120 g) yogurt
powdered sugar or honey
a little lemon juice

Strawberry Sauce:
½ lb (250 g) strawberries
just under
⅔ cup (80 g) powdered
sugar
juice of ¼ lemon

Strawberry Yogurt Parfait: Wash and trim strawberries, puree (**Note:** Reserve a few nice whole berries for garnish) and stir together with lemon juice and yogurt until smooth. Whip cream until creamy and refrigerate. Stir eggs with yolks, granulated and vanilla sugars, and salt in a mixing bowl and beat over steam to a creamy consistency, all the while rotating the mixing bowl and beating rapidly so that no lumps form. Remove mixing bowl from heat once the cream is hot, "beat cold" (beat until the mixture is cooled to room temperature). Then stir ⅓ of the whipping cream with the yogurt-strawberry mixture firmly into the egg mixture. Carefully fold in remaining whipped cream into the cream. Pour the mixture into small molds and freeze covered with foil for at least 6 hours.

Yogurt Sauce: Stir yogurt with sugar or honey and lemon juice until smooth and chill.

Strawberry Sauce: Wash and trim the strawberries and drain well, puree with powdered sugar, and press through a sieve. Flavor sauce with lemon juice and powdered sugar to taste.

Turn out strawberry parfait onto plates, garnish with the sauces and strawberries, and serve.

Ice Cream Auflauf with Herb Liqueur

Wrap 8 small casserole dishes with baking paper or parchment wrapping paper so that the paper sticks up about 3 inches above the edge. Fix with adhesive tape (Illustration).

Pour whipping cream into a bowl and freeze until the cream on the edge of the bowl is starting to ice over. Then slowly beat the cream with an electric mixer at low speed and put back in the refrigerator.

Stir egg yolks together with granulated and vanilla sugars, 3 tbsp water, and salt in a mixing bowl and beat over steam to a creamy consistency, all the while rotating the mixing bowl and beating rapidly so that no lumps form. Remove mixing bowl from heat once the cream is hot, "beat cold" (beat until the mixture is cooled to room temperature). Then stir $1/3$ of the whipped cream and the herb liqueur firmly into the egg mixture. Carefully fold in remaining whipped cream into the cream. Pour the mixture up to ¾ inch (2 cm) above the edge of the prepared dishes, knock them on the work surface so that parfait is distributed evenly, cover with foil, and freeze for at least 6 hours.

Before serving, remove the paper strips and sprinkle parfait with cocoa. Serve in the dish, if desired with cookies.

Tip: For an Ice Cream *Souffle* Grand Marnier, use Grand Marnier instead of herb liqueur.

Yields 8 servings

a little over 2 cups (½ l) whipping cream
4 egg yolks
²⁄₃ cup (120 g) granulated sugar
1 tsp vanilla sugar
pinch of salt
3-4 tbsp herb liqueur
cocoa

Poppy Seed Parfait with Rum Berries

Yields 6 servings

Poppy Seed Parfait:
a little over 2 cups (½ l)
whipping cream
¾ cup (150 g)
granulated sugar
1 tsp vanilla sugar
pinch of salt
a little under ¼ cup (30 g)
gray poppy seeds, finely
ground
1 egg
4 egg yolks

Rum Berries:
1 lb (400 g) mixed berries
powdered sugar
4 cl (2–3 tbsp) rum

Heat whipping cream with ½ of the granulated sugar, vanilla sugar, salt, and poppy seeds (do not boil!). Stir eggs with yolks and remaining granulated sugar in a mixing bowl and beat over steam to a creamy consistency with a whisk, all the while rotating the mixing bowl and beating rapidly so that no lumps form. Remove mixing bowl from the heat as soon as the cream is hot.

Stir poppy seeds into the egg mixture and slowly heat to 175°F (80°C) while constantly stirring. Then puree mixture with a hand blender and let cool in a cold water bath to room temperature, stirring repeatedly. Cover with plastic wrap and refrigerate about 12 hours (don't freeze!).

Remove cream from the refrigerator and beat in mixer at low speed until stiff. Pour parfait mixture into 6 ramekins (or into a *Rehrücken* form or parfait form lined with plastic wrap), cover with foil, and freeze for at least six hours. Briefly dip ramekins (or form) in hot water, turn out onto cold plates (or cut into slices and place on plates), and serve with rum berries.

Rum Berries: Wash and trim berries and drain well. Place fruit in a bowl, sprinkle with powdered sugar, drizzle with rum, and mix well. Cover with plastic wrap and let stand for about 2–3 hours.

Basic Recipes for *Sauces*

Applesauce

Yields 6–8 servings

¾ lb (350 g) apples
(e.g., Elstar, Jonagold)
¼ cup ($^1/_{16}$ l) white wine or
water juice of 1 lemon
about ½ cup minus
1 tbsp (80 g) granulated
sugar
1 small cinnamon stick
some apple brandy

Wash apples, peel, quarter, core, and cut apples into quarters. Bring ¼ cup ($^1/_{16}$ l) of water to a boil with white wine, lemon juice, granulated sugar, cinnamon stick, and several apple peels. (**Note:** The apple peels lend the cooking broth a much more intensive taste.) Then remove the peels from the broth, add the apple quarters into the broth, and cook until soft. Remove from the heat and puree the apples in the broth with a hand blender. Let applesauce cool and season with apple brandy.

Strawberry Sauce

Yields about 4 servings

1 cup (150 g) strawberries
a little over
$^1/_3$ cup (50 g) powdered
sugar
juice of ¼ lemon

Wash and trim the strawberries and drain well; puree with powdered sugar and lemon juice.

Bilberry Sauce

Yields about 1 ¼ cup
(300 ml)

1 $^1/_3$ cup (200 g) bilberries,
sorted, washed
$^1/_3$ cup (70 g) granulated
sugar

Bring a heaping cup (100 g) bilberries to a boil with just shy of 2 ¾ tbsp (40 ml) of water and granulated sugar, puree well with a hand blender, return to a boil. Add remaining bilberries, swirl, and let cool.

Raspberry Sauce

Yields about ¼ liter

2 cups (250 g) raspber-
ries almost ½ cup (60 g)
powdered sugar

Wash raspberries, drain well, and puree them with sugar; strain through a sieve.

Basic Recipes for *Sauces*

Yields 4 servings

1 ¼ tbsp (10 g) vanilla
pudding powder
 (or cornstarch)
½ cup (⅛ l) strong coffee
1 egg yolk
½ cup (⅛ l) coffee cream
(15% fat)
⅓ cup (70 g) granulated
sugar
1 tsp vanilla sugar
pinch of salt

Coffee Sauce

Stir together vanilla pudding powder with a little coffee
and egg yolk. Bring the remaining coffee to a boil with
the coffee cream, granulated and vanilla sugars, and salt.
Stir in the coffee-yolk mixture and cook, stirring constantly, until the sauce is creamy. **Tip:** The sauce may be kept
warm over steam.

Yields about 1 ¼ cup (300 ml)

2 tsp vanilla pudding
powder
1 cup (¼ l) milk
¾ cup of granulated sugar

Caramel Sauce

Stir vanilla pudding powder with some cold milk until
smooth; heat remaining milk to about 175°F (80°C). Heat
a pan, lightly brown about ¼ of the sugar, add another ¼
of the sugar (reduce heat if necessary), and caramelize
until light brown; continue until all of the sugar is used up
and lightly browned. Immediately douse with half of the
milk mixture. **Careful:** The milk will boil up strongly, so
the pan must be fairly large. Pour in remaining milk. Let
stand until the caramel is completely dissolved. (It may
be necessary to puree with a hand blender until no more
lumps are present.) Add vanilla pudding milk and cook
while constantly stirring until a creamy sauce results.

Yields about 1 cup (¼ l)

1 cup (¼ l) milk
3 ⅓ tbsp (40 g) granulated
sugar
1 tsp vanilla sugar
pinch of salt
1 ¼ tbsp (10 g) vanilla
pudding powder
1 egg yolk
1 shot of almond liqueur

Almond Sauce

Bring a little over ¾ cup (³/₁₆ l) milk to a boil with granulated and vanilla sugars and salt. Stir remaining milk with
vanilla pudding powder and the egg yolk until smooth
and pour into the boiling milk while stirring. Refine sauce
with almond liqueur to taste.

Basic Recipes for *Sauces*

Apricot Sauce

Yields 6 servings

$^2/_3$ lb (300 g) apricots
$^1/_3$ cup plus
1 tbsp (80 g) granulated sugar
juice of ½ lemon
½ cinnamon stick

Wash apricots, core, quarter, and bring to a boil with ¼ cup ($^1/_{16}$ l) water and the remaining ingredients; cook apricots until soft. Remove cinnamon stick and puree sauce. **Note:** If desired, season to taste with lemon juice and sugar.

Cranberry Sauce

Yields about 6 servings

2 ½ cups (250 g) cranberries
1 $^1/_8$ cup (150 g) powdered sugar

Select the best cranberries, wash, trim, stir slowly with powdered sugar in a mixer for about 10 minutes and let stand. Repeat this procedure until the sugar is completely dissolved.

Currant Sauce

Yields 6 servings

150 g Ribiseln
80 g Staubzucker
3 cl (2 EL) Johannisbeerlikör (Crème de Cassis)

Wash currants, remove stems, bring to a boil with ¼ cup ($^1/_{16}$ l) water, powdered sugar, cinnamon stick, puree briefly (**Note:** The seeds should stay whole, pureed seeds make the sauce bitter). Pass currant puree through a sieve, stir together with liqueur, and chill.
Tip: Black currant sauce is made the same way.

Chocolate Sauce 1

Yields about $^7/_8$ cup (200 ml)

1 tsp vanilla sugar
½ cup (100 g) granulated sugar
1 cup (100 g) dark chocolate couverture
1 tbsp rum

Bring just under ¼ cup (50 ml) water to a boil with vanilla and granulated sugars; remove from heat, stir in chocolate and rum. Briefly blend with a hand blender and let cool slightly.

Chocolate Sauce 2

Yields about 1 $^2/_3$ cup (400 ml)

a little over 1 cup (250 ml) whipping cream
a little over ¾ cup (80 g) milk chocolate couverture
1 ¼ cup (120 g) dark chocolate couverture

Bring whipping cream to a boil, chop both couvertures coarsely, stir in, and let melt. Briefly blend chocolate sauce with a hand blender and keep warm.

258

Basic Recipes for Sauces

Yields 5 servings

1 vanilla pod
1 cup (¼ l) milk
¹/₃ cup (60 g) granulated sugar
pinch of salt
1 ¼ tbsp (10 g) vanilla pudding powder
1 egg yolk

1 tbsp (10 g) cornstarch
a little over 1 cup (250 ml) white wine (Riesling)
½ cup minus
1 tbsp (80 g) granulated sugar
1 small stick of cinnamon
peel of 1 lemon (untreated)
½ lb (250 g) seedless grapes, washed and trimmed

Yields 6 servings

1 ½ tbsp (10 g) vanilla pudding powder
1 cup (¼ l) milk
1 egg yolk
¹/₃ cup (70 g) granulated sugar
pinch of salt
2 cl (1–2 tbsp) Williams brandy

Yields 6 servings

1 cup (¼ l) milk
¹/₃ cup (70 g) granulated sugar
1 tsp vanilla sugar
salt cinnamon sticks
10 g (about 1 tsp) vanilla pudding powder
1 egg yolk

Vanilla Sauce

Cut vanilla pod lengthwise. Bring ¼ cup (¹/₁₆ l) milk with sugar, vanilla pod, and salt to a boil. Stir remaining milk with vanilla pudding powder and egg yolk until smooth and pour into the boiling milk while stirring. Remove vanilla pod.

Wine Sauce

Stir cornstarch with a little white wine until smooth. Bring remaining ingredients (except the grapes) to a boil. Stir in cornstarch and boil until it thickens. Remove cinnamon stick and lemon peel. Add grapes, return to a boil, and remove from heat.

Williams Sauce

Stir vanilla pudding mix with a little cold milk and egg yolk until smooth. Bring remaining milk with sugar and salt to a boil. Pour vanilla-yolk milk into boiling milk while stirring, cook until creamy while stirring constantly. Allow to cool, stir in Williams brandy. Puree the sauce with a hand blender. **Note:** If the sauce is too thin, possibly add a little whipped cream and stir until it thickens.

Cinnamon Sauce

Bring ¼ cup (¹/₁₆ l) of milk to a boil with granulated and vanilla sugars, salt, and cinnamon sticks, remove from heat and let stand for about 10 minutes. Blend remaining milk with vanilla pudding powder and egg yolk. Remove cinnamon sticks from milk, bring to a boil again, and stir the vanilla egg yolk milk into the cinnamon milk. Cook sauce, constantly stirring, until the sauce thickens. Allow to cool and chill.

Blend cinnamon sauce with a hand blender before serving.

Basic Recipes for *Compotes*

Apple Compote

Yields 4 servings

3 apples (for example, Elstar, Golden Delicious)
juice and peel of 1 lemon (untreated)
½ cup (¹/₈ l) white wine (dry)
½ cinnamon stick
3–4 cloves
¼ cup (50 g) granulated sugar

Wash apples, peel, core, and cut into eighths. Drizzle apples with lemon juice. Bring ½ cup (¹/₈ l) water to a boil with remaining lemon juice, lemon peel, white wine, cinnamon stick, cloves, and granulated sugar. Cover and cook apples until soft; let apple compote cool slightly.

Stewed Apricots

Yields 6 servings

2 ½ heaping cups (400 g) apricots
²/₃ cup (120 g) granulated sugar
3 cl (2 tbsp) apricot brandy
peel and juice of ½ lemon (untreated) lemon zest
½ cinnamon stick

Wash apricots, halve, remove pits, and cut into slices. Bring just shy of 2 ¾ tbsp (40 ml) of water to a boil with sugar, lemon juice and zest, cinnamon, and apricot brandy. Add apricot slices, cover, and cook over low heat until soft. Be careful not to overcook! **Note:** The alcohol can also be omitted.

Poached Pears

Yields 4 servings

4 pears (preferably Bartlett)
²/₃ cup (120 g) granulated sugar
juice of 1 lemon
4 cl (2–3 tbsp) Williams brandy

Wash pears, peel, halve, remove seeds. Bring granulated sugar to a boil with lemon juice, Williams brandy and a little over 1 ½ cups (³/₈ l) water. Put in pear halves and cook until al dente. Let pears cool in the broth; then remove, drain well, and if desired, cut into thin slices.

Basic Recipes for *Compotes*

Yields 5 servings

1 tbsp (10 g) cornstarch
a little over 1 cup (250 ml)
red wine
½ cup minus
1 tbsp (80 g) granulated
sugar
1 small cinnamon stick
1 piece of lemon
peel ½ lb (250 g)
stemmed, pitted cherries or
sour cherries

Red Wine Cherries

Stir together cornstarch with a little red wine. Bring remaining ingredients, except the cherries, to a boil and thicken the broth by stirring in the cornstarch. Remove cinnamon stick and lemon peel, add cherries, and bring to a boil again.

Tip: Instead of fresh cherries or sour cherries, jarred (canned) fruit can also be used. Strain and drain well.

Yields 8 servings (as a side)

about 1 ⅓ lb (600 g)
plums
¾ cup (150 g) granulated
sugar
juice of ½ lemon
1 cinnamon stick
1 tsp plum brandy
(slivovitz)

Stewed Plums

Wash plums, core, and quarter them, then bring to a boil with remaining ingredients; cover and stew until soft. Remove cinnamon stick, add slivovitz, and let the stewed plums cool.

Basic Recipes for Doughs, Batters,

Baumkuchen

Yields 1 pan (9 ½ inches
x 12 inches x 1 ½ inches
[24cm x 30cm x 4cm])

1 ¹/₈ cup (250 g) butter
7 eggs
1 ¹/₈ cup (200 g) raw
marzipan heaping
²/₃ cup (100 g) powdered
sugar
2 tsp vanilla sugar
zest of ½ lemon
pinch of salt
just under ½ cup (70 g)
cornstarch
¾ cup (150 g) granulated
sugar
1 ¹/₈ cup (110 g) flour
(fine)

Cut butter into small pieces let soften at room temperature.

Separate eggs. Stir yolks with raw marzipan until smooth. Add powdered and vanilla sugars, lemon zest and salt, and stir until creamy.

Add butter and cornstarch and beat creamy. Beat egg whites with granulated sugar until stiff. Stir together ¹/₃ of the egg whites with the yolk mixture; carefully fold in remaining egg whites alternating with flour.

Line pan with aluminum foil. Spread *Baumkuchen* batter as thinly as possible (no more than ¹/₁₀ inch [3 mm] high) into the pan and briefly bake in a preheated oven at 500°F (250°C) broil setting until lightly browned. Remove from the oven, apply another thin layer, and bake until golden brown. Repeat process until all of the batter is used up and baked.

Tip for storage: *Baumkuchen* can be stored without loss of quality for 2 weeks in the refrigerator wrapped in plastic wrap, frozen even longer.

Butter Crumbles

2 ½ cups (250 g) flour
(fine)
a heaping ¾ cup (180 g)
butter, cut into small cubes
¹/₃ cup (60 g) raw
marzipan, cut into small
cubes
heaping ²/₃ cup (100 g)
powdered sugar
pinch of baking powder
¹/₃ package vanilla sugar
pinch of salt
pinch of cinnamon

Quickly knead all of the ingredients together and work into crumbles between your fingers. Chill for about 10 minutes, then place crumbles on a baking sheet lined with parchment paper, and bake in a preheated oven at 325°-350°F (165–170°C) for about 18–20 minutes until golden brown. While still hot chop to desired size with a spatula (dough scraper).

Crumbles, Frying Batters

Erdäpfelteig

Yields about 4 servings

about 1 lb (400 g) mealy
potatoes
1 cup (100 g) flour
(medium fine)
1 tbsp wheat semolina
pinch of salt
2 heaping tbsp (30 g)
butter
1 egg yolk

flour for preparing

Wash potatoes, boil, peel, and let cool for a bit and press
through a potato press while still hot. It should yield about
½ lb (250 g) of potato mixture. While still warm, quickly
work mixture of flour, semolina, salt, butter, and egg yolk
into a potato dough. Then follow the appropriate recipe.

Important: Always cook a sample. If the dough is too
soft, use a little flour or semolina to bring it to the right
consistency.

This dough is suitable for fruit *Knödel*, *Powidl* pockets (or
other fruit pockets), poppy seed, nut, bread crumb, or
semolina noodles.

Topfenteig

Yields about 6 servings

a little over ¼ cup (60 g)
soft butter
peel of ½ lemon
(untreated), zested
1 tsp vanilla sugar
pinch of salt
1 cup (250 g) Topfen (10%
fat), strained
1 egg
1 ½ cups (150 g) flour
(fine)

Stir together butter, lemon zest, vanilla sugar, and salt
until fluffy. Gradually stir in *Topfen* and egg. Finally,
rapidly stir in the flour. Pour *Topfenteig* onto parchment
paper, flatten, cover with plastic wrap, and let rest in the
refrigerator for about 1–2 hours.

The dough is wonderful for fruit *Knödel* (strawberry,
apricot, raspberry *Knödel*), *Topfen* pockets, and *Topfen*
noodles.

Yields 6 servings

2 eggs
1 ⅓ cup plus
1 tbsp (140 g) flour (fine)
½ cup (⅛ l) white wine
2 tbsp oil or
melted butter
peel of ½ lemon
(untreated), zested

Weinbackteig

Separate eggs. Stir together flour with white wine, oil,
yolks, lemon zest, vanilla, and granulated sugars and salt
until smooth. If desired, puree dough with a hand blender
or strain through a sieve. Beat egg whites with granulated
sugar until stiff and fold in.

Variation: Prepare *Milchbackteig* or *Bierbackteig* the same
way, only instead of wine, use milk or beer.

Basic Recipes for *Creams*

Butter Cream

1 cup (¼ l) milk
1 cup (200 g) granulated
sugar
1 tsp vanilla sugar
pinch of salt
¼ cup (30 g) vanilla
pudding powder or
cornstarch
1 egg yolk
1 ¾ cup (400 g) butter

Bring ¼ cup ($^1/_{16}$ l) milk to a boil with ½ cup (100 g) granulated sugar, vanilla sugar, and salt. Stir remaining milk with vanilla pudding powder and egg yolk until smooth and pour into the boiling milk. While constantly stirring with a whisk, return to a boil and cook until the taste of the vanilla pudding powder has dissipated. Pour cream into a bowl and stir together with the remaining granulated sugar until it is lukewarm. Stir in ½ cup (100 g) butter and continue stirring, preferably with an electric mixer, until the cream has cooled to room temperature (= "beating cold"). Stir in remaining butter until fluffy. Use butter cream or chill, prior to use, stir until creamy.

Paris Cream

Yields about 3 ¾ cups
(600 g)

3 cups (300 g) dark
chocolate couverture
1 ¼ cup (300 g) whipping
cream
$^1/_3$ cup (80 g) hazelnut
cream

Chop couverture chocolate into small pieces. Bring whipping cream to a boil, remove from heat, add chocolate, and stir until it is completely melted. Add the hazelnut cream and puree the mixture for about 1 minute with a hand blender. Subsequently pour into a shallow container and let sit; the cream should thicken, but not solidify.

Vanilla Cream

Yields about 4 2/3 cups
(750 g)

a little over 2 cups
(½ l) milk
$^2/_3$ cup (120 g) granulated
sugar
2 tsp vanilla sugar
pinch of salt
¼ cup (40 g) vanilla
pudding powder or
cornstarch
2 egg yolks powdered
sugar

Bring ½ cup ($^1/_8$ l) milk to a boil with granulated and vanilla sugars and salt. Stir in remaining milk with vanilla pudding powder and egg yolks until smooth, stir into the boiling milk, and return to a boil, constantly stirring with a whisk, until the taste of the vanilla pudding powder has dissipated. Pour cream into a bowl, sprinkle with powdered sugar, and let cool. Cover with foil and chill.

Covered and chilled, the vanilla cream will last about 4 days without loss of quality.

Tempering Couverture

There are various methods of getting couverture ready for use that require a certain amount of experience and sensitivity.

1. Chop couverture (it is also available as chocolate chips). Slowly and evenly heat to a temperature of 91°F (33°C).
2. Melt the couverture in a water bath or the microwave, pour about ¾ of the couverture onto a stone slab, and table it with a spatula until the couverture begins to thicken (at about 77–79°F ([25–26°C]). Immediately stir in with the remaining couverture and heat carefully to 89–91°F (32–33°C).
3. Melt couverture, gradually add grated or chopped couverture, and stir until it begins to thicken (at about 77–79°F [25–26°C]). Then carefully heat to 89–91°F (32–33°C).

Tips:

♦ If there are still unbroken pieces in the couverture, carefully stir until smooth with a hand blender. (Note: no air bubbles!)
♦ In order to avoid changing the flavor, dark couverture should not be heated in excess of 122°F (50°C), milk and white couverture not above 104°F (40°C).
♦ In order to achieve optimum gloss, the cake or cookies should be at room temperature (70–72°F [21–22°C]) and the couverture should be around 88–91°F (31–33°C).
♦ If the couverture is too thick, it can be thinned with a little heated cocoa butter.

Instead of tempering couverture, you can use the following glaze: 1 cup (100 g) dark chocolate couverture, 1 cup (100 g) store-bought chocolate glaze or store-bought glaze mix, 1 ½ tbsp (20 g) coconut shortening.

Melt chocolate and chocolate glaze in a microwave oven or water bath (not above 104°F [40°C]); stir repeatedly, dissolve coconut shortening separately, and mix with the chocolate. Cool glaze to about 97–100°F (36–38°C) and use.

Bakeware

Gugelhupf, Rehrücken, Kranzkuchen, Reindling—without the correct baking pan, none of these cakes would have their characteristic appearance.

Baking molds have been used for several thousand years to give baked goods a specific shape. The original materials of the molds were stone, wood, clay, copper, and cast iron. Initially, animal and plant motifs served as models for baking molds, as did symbols from mythology and Christianity with ritual associations.

Starting in the Middle Ages, carved wooden models were also used. The dough pressed into these molds mirrored the smallest details of their baking molds' design.

Baking molds serve the purpose of "holding together" dough, protecting it from burning and giving baked goods a particular shape. They should also provide a good thorough baking and easy release of baked goods from the mold.

Today, a wide range of bakeware is available, but a few points should generally be observed when using baking molds:

- Colors affect baking time: Darker forms require a shorter cooking time than light forms of the same material and content. Dough browns in darker forms faster than in lighter ones.
- Dough needs longer to bake in forms with larger filling capacity than in smaller, flat shapes. In a loaf pan, the same amount of dough takes longer to bake than in a flat pan. Therefore, caution (!) when altering ingredient quantities.
- Never cut cakes and Tortes in coated forms, don't use sharp objects to scrape stuck-on cake pieces out of the mold.
- With glass forms, it is important to note that glass transmits heat very slowly but very evenly to baked goods and therefore—just as with ceramic and refractory porcelain forms—baking time must be extended.

Dariol Form:	For creams, Mohr im Hemd, puddings.
Gugelhupf Pan:	For baking blended doughs and heavy batters. In varying versions.
Pastry Frame:	Extendable frame, thus individually adjustable, for baking and inserting *Schnitten*.
Wreath Form:	For baking blended doughs and heavy batters; smooth or ribbed.
Fruit Torte Form:	For cakes, pies, quiches, round, smooth or ribbed, high or low.
Rehrücken Pan:	For baking of short crust doughs; conical or round.
Schaumrollen Mold:	For wrapping with *Blätterteig* for *Schaumrollen*, etc., pointed, slightly conical, or straight.
Spring Form:	For lateral opening, with different uses.
Torte Rings:	In different sizes and heights, adjustable for baking; in plastic for using with cream Tortes.

Special Terms

Glaze	thinly brush gingerbread, fruit, macaroons with sugar solution or Torte jelly.
Stem	remove or pluck stems from berries. Roll out dough with a rolling pin. Dampfl a pre-ferment (pre-dough) out of yeast.
Fondant	concentrated sugar solution for glazing pastries, available in specialty pastry shops (confectioner's).
Clarified butter	melt butter. Skim rising foam from the surface .
Beating cold	remove mixture that has been beaten warm over steam and continue to beat until the mixture has reached room temperature.
Sugar Solution (***Läuterzucker***)	bring water and sugar to a boil in a 1:1 ratio and chill. Sugar solution can be stored in a closed container in the refrigerator for a few weeks.
Blend	carefully blend different ingredients.
Strain	strain fruits, Topfen, or creams through a sieve or strainer.
Souffle-ing (***Soufflieren***)	rise full of air.
Pierce (***Stupfen***)	pierce Mürbteig or Blätterteig with a fork several times to prevent the formation of bubbles and irregular rising of the dough during baking.
Tabling	working sugar heated to a certain degree on the edge of a mixing bowl or a marble slab. Melted couverture is also tabled on marble for proper processing. See illustration, p. 265.
Couverture:	Austrian name for couverture is Tunkmasse (dipping mixture). A very fine chocolate with low sugar and a high cocoa content. A distinction is made between dark, milk, and white couverture and special kinds.

1 egg = 50 g | 1 egg yolk = 20 g | 1 egg white = 30 g

Glossary

Apfelnockerln	Thick soft apple dumplings, see also *Nockerln*.
Arme Ritter	conventional German term for what we call French toast, literally translating as "poor knight", as in that was all they could afford to eat!
Auflauf	Sweet or savory casserole dish.
Backteig	Frying batter.
Bananenschnitten	*Bananen* = bananas, see *Schnitten*.
Baumkuchen	A traditional layered cake, literally "tree cake", the name deriving from the characteristic rings that appear when sliced.
Beugel	Austrian baked good similar to our bagel.
Biedermeier era	The era characterized by the middle-class sensibilities of the period between 1815 and 1848.
Biskottes	Sponge cake fingers.
Biskuit	Not the same as "biscuit"! The closest approximation is a "sponge cake", see chapter on the etymology of the word and the development of the *Biskuit* from hard biscuit to airy pastry dough.
Blätterteig	literally "leaf dough", comparable to phylo dough or puff pastry dough), a simple pastry dough that is layered with fat (if butter is used it is known as *Butterteig*), folded and rolled out again
Brandteig	Literally "burned dough", type of pastry dough comparable to choux pastry.
Brandteigkrapfen	*Krapfen* made from *Brandteig*, see *Krapfen*, *Brandteig*.
Buchtel	Sweet baked dumplings made of yeast dough.
Buchteln	Yeast dumplings.
Butterteig	see *Blätterteig*
Charlotte	A cream dessert where sponge cake or cookies are used to line a mold which is then filled with custard or fruit puree.
Cremeschnitten	*Creme* = cream, see *Schnitten*.
Dalken	Another type of Austrian pancake of Eastern European origin.
Dampfl	Austrian term for the pre-ferment test dough.
Erdäpfelteig	Potato dough (Austrian term for potatoes translates literally as "earth apples").
Faschingskrapfen	Carnival doughnuts.
Florentiner	Literally "Florentine", almond and chocolate cookies.
Fruchtplunder	Fruit danishes, see *Plunder*.
Germknödel	Fluffy yeast dough dumpling filled with plum jam and topped with poppy seeds and vanilla sauce or melted butter.
Germpalatschinken	A type of *Palatschinken* prepared with yeast (Germ) dough.
Golatschen	Kolache pastries, originally a semi-sweet dessert from Eastern Europe, made from yeast dough with a variety of fillings.
Granatapfel	Pomegranate
Grießknödel	Semolina dumplings, see also *Knödel*.
Grießschmarren	Semolina *Schmarren*, see also *Schmarren*.
Grillage Torte	*Grillage* is an Austrian mixture of melted sugar and chopped nuts similar to brittle.
Guglhupf or Gugelhupf	Austrian term for marble or bundt cake.

Heidelbeeren	Bilberries, often confused with ordinary blueberries, which work fine as a substitute.
Herren Torte	*Herr* is German for Mister or man, hence: Men's Torte.
Indianerkrapfen	Indian doughnuts.
Jause	Austrian term for "snacktime".
Kapuzinerknödel	The *Kapuzinerknödel* (Capuchin dumplings) get their name from their resemblance to monkish tonsures
Kardinalschnitten	*Kardinal* = cardinal, see *Schnitten*.
Kärntner Reindling	Traditional Easter cake made of yeast dough
Kipferln	Austrian term for small crescent-shaped cookies.
Klößer	See *Knödel*
Knödel	Dumplings, sweet or savory
Koch	Porridge dish rich in fat.
Krapfen	Fried pastry, similar to donuts, often filled.
Krapferln	The Austrian diminutive form for *Krapfen*, i.e. little *Krapfen*, see also *Krapfen*.
Marillenknödel	Apricot dumplings, see also *Knödel*
Mehlspeisen	Literally "flour dishes", term encompassing not only pastries but also breads, cakes, cookies and biscuits - anything made with flour in other words!
Mohnkoch	Poppy seed pudding, see also *Koch*.
Mohnzopf	Poppy seed plait.
Mohr im Hemd	Literally "Moor in a Shirt", a type of chocolate pudding.
Mürbteig	Austrian dough similar to shortcrust pastry dough.
Nockerln	Thick soft dumplings, comparable to the Italian *gnocchi*, served sweet or savory in the Austrian kitchen.
Nusstaler	The Taler (English: Thaler) was a silver coin in use in much of Europe for four hundred years; the Nut Thaler is a round walnut cookie.
Omelette	No eggs here, this is another type of Austrian pancake.
Omelettenteig	Batter for *Omeletten* pancakes, see also *Omelette*.
Palatschinken	A type of pancake with Eastern European roots, has nothing to do with ham ("*Schinken*")!
Palatschinkenteig	Batter for *Palatschinken* pancakes, see also *Palatschinken*.
Pariserspitze	Descriptive name for a pastry translating as "peaks of Paris".
Pfannkuchen	The traditional German term (as opposed to Austrian) for pancake, its literal translation.
Plunder	Danish pastries, often with glazed fruit, see also *Plunderteig*
Plunderteig	Dough similar to Danish pastry dough.
Pofesen	Austrian fried pastry.
Potizen	Sweet bread with nut filling of Eastern European origin.
Powidl	Eastern European plum jam (from the Czech *povidla*), very popular in Austria both as a spread and as a pastry filling
Ranftl	Austrian term for a uniform white ring that appears on fried *Krapfen*.
Rehrücken	Literally "saddle of venison", which a well-known Austrian pastry resembles that is baked in a mold giving it a curved shape.

Rigó Jancischnitten	A chocolate cream *Schnitte* named after a gypsy violinist, see also *Schnitten*.
Schaumauflauf	Cream casserole, also known as a *Souffle*
Schaumrollen	Literally "cream rolls", hollow *Blätterteig* pastries filled with cream, see also *Blätterteig*.
Schaumschnitten	Cream cakes, see also *Schnitten*.
Scheiterhaufen with **Schneehaube**	*D*escriptive term for the visual appearance of this dish: the *Scheiterhaufen* was the stake where heretics or witches were burnt, and *Schneehaube* literally means "Snow Cover".
Schlosserbuben	Literally "locksmith boys", a type of Austrian fried pastry.
Schmarren	A traditional Austrian shredded pancake; also the word for "nonsense".
Schmarrenteig	Batter for a *Schmarren* pancake, see also *Schmarren*.
Schnee	Literally "snow", used in a few dishes as a descriptive term for egg whites beaten with sugar.
Schnitten	Literally "slices", the designation for flat and (usually) rectangular or square cakes, often layered.
Stanitzel	A sweet conical pastry stuffed with cream and fruits.
Steckerlobst	Literally "little stick fruit", candied fruit threaded on sticks.
Stollen	Traditional German or Austrian Christmas cake.
Teig	German term for dough, used throughout as a compound word such as *Blätterteig, Topfenteig, Mürbteig* etc.
Topfen	*Topfen* is the Austrian version of the German *Quark*, a type of curd cheese that can be used in dishes both sweet and savory.
Topfengolatschen	*Golatschen* made with *Topfen* dough, see also *Golatschen, Topfen*.
Topfenteig	A sweet dough made with plenty of *Topfen*.
Waldviertler Plum Knödel	Waldviertel is the northwestern region of the Austrian state of Lower Austria, see also *Knödel*.
Wäschermädel	Washing maids, a type of Austrian fried pastry.
Weinbackteig	Frying batter made with wine.
Williams brandy	An Austrian spirit distilled from *Williams* pears.
Williams Christ pears	The Austrian term for what we call Bartlett pears.
Zigeunerschnitten	Zigeuner = gypsy, see *Schnitten*.
Zopf	Plaited pastry.
Zwetschkenlatwerge	See *Powidl*.

Index